ENTERPRISING YOUNG MEN

The California Gold Rush Memoir
of Missourian
Robert Mason Clark

Marion County, Missouri

MARSHA K. CLARK

Editor, Compiler

Enterprising Young Men:
The California Gold Rush Memoir
of Robert Mason Clark

Edited and Compiled by
Marsha K. Clark

Published in the United States by
Marsha K. Clark

ISBN: 979-8-3306-0672-6

Cover, interior layout, and the map of RMC's journey
  designed by Brad Cook.
Images used on the cover or within the interior are
  public domain or were provided by the family.

Based on the 1970 compilation prepared by Edna Clark
Hoxworth, using copies of R.M. Clark's account of his gold
mining aspirations as they appeared in weekly features of
the Hunnewell Graphic newspaper (Missouri) in 1903.

"My mind was back to my old home with my old
companions that I had left behind. Whilst I sat there
musing, a middle aged gentleman stepped up beside our
wagon and printed on our wagon sheet, in big letters,
these words:

SUCCESS TO THE ENTERPRISING YOUNG MEN

I looked up at the printing... and I felt better. It gave me
new energy. Even after, when I would get down in spirits
or in hard places, I would look on the printing, and it
would man me up."

Robert M. Clark on his way west April 9, 1850,
Old Bloomington, Macon County, Missouri

Contents

Appendices

PREFACE

In the Spring of 1903 through November 20 of that year, the *Hunnewell Graphic* newspaper ran a series of long, two-column accounts written by Robert Mason Clark titled "R. M. Clark's Journey Across the Plains, the Overland Route to California." These segments detailed Clark's adventures to the California Gold Rush in 1850 at age twenty-one and his return to Northeast Missouri at almost twenty-three. At the time of the printed columns, Robert "Bob" Clark was seventy-four years old. He lost his diary a few months before arriving back at his Marion County home on January 28, 1852. Clark died April 28, 1917, at age eighty-eight years, six months and ten days.

A determined effort by this editor to locate all the original print copies of the printed series was unsuccessful. No copies of the *Graphic's* series of the progenitor's gold rush memoir were known to exist within the circle of descendants from Robert Clark's son Samuel Wilson Clark, who is my husband's grandfather. In 1970, Samuel Wilson Clark's daughter, Edna L. (Clark) Hoxworth, was fortunate to have borrowed copies of the serial columns retained by some cousins. Undertaking an arduous project, Edna sat before a typewriter to compile all columns as one document.

Edna most likely used carbon sheets to create three or four copies for family members. Her nephew, Richard Clark, relayed to this editor Edna typed the series compilation twice to create additional copies for other family members, possibly using spirit duplicator (mimeograph) masters the second time; it isn't known.

Her typing tasks were performed before the years when xerography was widely accessible to the public.

I was able to resuscitate Robert Clark's adventures for another century thanks to the retyping done by Edna Hoxworth and discovering microfilmed copies of the *Hunnewell Graphic* held in the Newspaper Collection of The State Historical Society of Missouri. For the year 1903, the Newspaper Collection holds only *Hunnewell Graphic* issues of August through December. The August 7 issue— the earliest issue available—begins with the gold seekers ("argonauts") traveling across the Black Hills of California. One can assume that Clark's memoir began appearing in the June or July issues of the newspaper.

The *Hunnewell Graphic's* typeset version includes several reading challenges. There are run-on sentences and phrases without the help of paragraph breaks, making the concepts difficult to grasp upon first reading. Likewise, Mrs. Hoxworth's typing structure reflects the *Hunnewell Graphic* account. The lines run from left margin to right margin without breaks, alternating from using all capital letters (for ease in accomplishing the massive task, one can assume) to traditional sentence format. Using double spacing on most pages and single spacing on others, her compilation totaled fifty-seven pages and was completed on October 4, 1970, in Edna's sixty-ninth year.

The edited and reformatted account that follows strives to create a version that is more likely to be read and easier for readers to engage with the adventurers and their times. Assuming the newspaper presented Clark's account accurately (and the typesetters may have applied their own phrasings and spellings), the nuances of Robert Clark's dialect, personality, and choice of words—including those recognized now as offensive, though used as accepted terminology within Clark's arena—are retained. Much of the improper grammar preserves the manner of speaking at that time. Some punctuation and spellings have been altered to enable ease of reading. Reading aids, such as footnotes to provide additional information, are included to bring a deeper understanding of things mentioned by Robert Clark.

Readers might stumble on the word emigrants, which is

frequently found throughout. It was common then to refer to 49ers as emigrants and subsequently still used by historians, noting that floods of people left their homes to seek riches in gold country.

Supplements are provided to help organize and clarify certain activities, people, relationships, places, and events. The bulk of what is provided as supplemental information comes from secondary sources; therefore, errors are certainly possible.

It is not the goal of this compilation to retell all that the 1848-1860s gold fever and decades following contributed to establishing Western settlements. There is a plethora of material published about the Gold Rush era that one can consult; many of these are included in the Bibliography. Atop this, I relied upon my general education, love for lifelong learning, curiosity about times past, and multiple undertakings to build family ties and histories through genealogy to carry this work from a vision to a completed volume.

By reading this expanded version of Robert Clark's account of that period, the reader can gain deeper and broader insight into the arduous pursuits and social schema that shaped the development of the western United States in the mid-1800s, especially that of Northeast Missouri. For the descendants of these argonauts, developing a greater appreciation for the intelligence and character of their adventurous, courageous, and ambitious Missouri ancestors will be gratifying.

- M.K.C.

EDITING NOTES FOR
THE READER

In addition to footnotes and appendices, some reader assists in this edited compilation are provided to expand understanding of activities, people, relationships, places, events and historical practices. The following notes about text treatments should be kept in mind.

TREATMENT	PURPOSE
Italicization	Italics highlight Robert Clark's reflections about life from the vantage of seventy-four years of age, separating them from the trip details.
Paragraph Breaks	To make reading easier, this edited version added frequent paragraph breaks. The *Hunnewell Graphic* used breaks although paragraphs were lengthy. The Hoxworth typing was mainly all capital letters without any paragraph breaks.
Quotations	Wherever Robert Clark's words clearly are dialogue, this edited version places those words in quotation marks for easier reading.

Colloquialisms   Corrections and footnote comments have been added where necessary to convey Robert Clark's obvious intentions. However, most misspellings, eye-dialect, and grammar have been retained as typed in the original transcript document prepared by Mrs. Hoxworth and as found in the microfilm copies of the *Hunnewell Graphic.*

Phrasing   Changes to the phrases were made where it would be helpful to add an article, conjunction, or pronoun, as well as phrasing marks (periods, commas, semicolons, colons, and dashes) for clarity. Some phrases were repositioned within a sentence to assist in understanding. Commas after introductory adverbials (e.g., *So, Well, Finally,* etc.) were not used in Clark's account; however, they have been added to enable reading ease. Compound adjectives (e.g. *rosy-cheeked, middle-aged, twenty-two; two-inch board*) were not hyphenated in the Hunnewell Graphic serial; however, the hyphen has been added where needed for reading clarity.

Sic   This abbreviation for the Latin *sic erat scriptum* indicates the preceding word(s) or spelling(s) are as they appear in the source. They retain the sentiment of the sentence as it appeared in the *Hunnewell Graphic* or Hoxworth version.

Map of Robert Mason Clark's Journey

INTRODUCTION

The year 1903 was poised for many reflection events and writings about westward activity in the United States. It marked the centennial of the preparation of Lewis and Clark's pursuit of a cross-country route to the Pacific Ocean that commenced after an 1893-94 winter, camped near the shores of the Mississippi at today's Wood River, Illinois. It was the year that the automobile was tested in a race to see which adventurer might successfully drive the four-wheeled machine from the West Coast to New York—the first cross-country automobile road trip. America was positioned to appreciate the story of mankind caught between an era of pastoralism and surging industrialization in pursuit of material wealth.

On June 20, 1903, *The Saturday Evening Post* began its serial of Jack London's *The Call of the Wild*, about the survival of the fittest. While most recognize London's story as a classic dog's tale, it is also a picture of the 1890s gold rush in Klondike, where London had journeyed amidst its harsh elements and pursuit of financial success through Alaskan gold mines in 1897.

Also in that notable year, the *Hunnewell Graphic*, a newspaper serving the populations within and around Shelby County in Northeast Missouri, told of another adventure about the bounding West, of prairie schooners and walking and riding 1800 miles under the spell of mining for gold. In a serial format, 1850s Missouri-to-California emigrant Robert Mason Clark, a resident reared on the farms of Marion County, recounted his man-versus-nature and man-versus-man journey.[1]

---

1 Hunnewell is a small village in neighboring Shelby County, Missouri. Hunnewell's newspaper served the area from 1886-1957. (Library of Congress, Directory of U.S. Newspapers in American Libraries)

Along with his brother Sam and four others from that adventurous region—Mike Heckard, Carson Gatewood, Henley Maddox and Frank See—Robert Clark crossed the plains of North America along the historic California Trail to seek success by way of hard labor and exploration.

This was a dream shared by thousands. Hearing accounts of other Missourians who left the plows and barns to heal gold fever, these six men, unencumbered in their early twenties, left the security of family and familiarity to seek fortunes that might alter their present trials and secure their futures. Both of the Clark brothers returned to tell of their trials, joys, and discoveries as shared in the following pages.

The discovery of gold and the rush that followed in 1849 arrived in the thrashing wake of many political revolutions that flooded Europe in 1848. That was also the year of the American women's call for suffrage at the Seneca Falls Convention. The Fugitive Slave Act, passed in 1850, inspired American abolitionist Harriet Beecher Stowe to compose a serial, later published as the book *Uncle Tom's Cabin*, which kindled the dawning of a war that ripped asunder the young nation of states a decade later. Men and women, young and old, awakened to new hungers. Things to discover and opportunities that determine one's fate arose as conditions changed.

Many early settlers of Marion County, Missouri—where Bob and Sam Clark were raised—emigrated there in the 1830s with other families from Kentucky, believing the land around Palmyra and Marion City near Mississippi River shores offered promise for prosperity. It was a time of ambition and dreams, and drive to fulfill them. Among these enthusiastic individuals was John Lewis Robards, who at age eleven in 1849 ventured across the plains to California with his father. A company of fifteen from Hannibal made that westward journey alongside the Robards. John Robards later noted in his collection of memorable life events that an impressionable fourteen-year-old Sam Clemens (Mark Twain), whose family also came to Missouri from Kentucky, was among the lads who gathered around Robards and his party of men, oxen, and wagons to wish them well on their westward journey. By 1861, at the age of twenty-three, Clemens, too, sought adventure in the mines of Nevada, traveling alongside his brother Orion by wagon.[2] It was this period during which

---

2 Orion was appointed Secretary of the Nevada territory, a patronage assignment in gratitude for "stumping" for Abraham Lincoln in the 1860 presidential election. Younger brother Sam traveled alongside to seek wealth.

he wrote humorous accounts that reflected his native Hannibal and times as a miner under his famous pen name.

The early twentieth century–when Robert Clark and Jack London released their reflections on paper in 1903–was an era of pastoralism. Writings and lectures reflected the critical essence of familiarity with nature, ushered by Robert Frost's poetry. It was also a time of industry, which was changing the ways of labor, livelihood, transportation, and communication. Clark's accounts of his Plains travel and mining adventures, and of the challenges and thrills of returning by ocean, reveal a time when one was deeply connected to nature and equally aware of it as an adversary. Writing of this at age seventy-four, in his gold rush memoir printed in the *Hunnewell Graphic* newspaper in the small Marion County, Missouri, community of Hunnewell, Robert Clark reminisced on crossing the desert northwest of Salt Lake in Utah forty-two years prior:[3]

> "Little did I then think that I would live to know that the [train] cars would pass through that country daily or that my children would inhabit it, for the general opinion with us then was that it was fit for nothing, (only)…buffalo and wild animals."

> "Clad so heavy in her native forests abounding in wild game and honey, the prairies adorned in summer time with native grass and set as with wild flowers. Here the wild deer loved to feed, sport, and play. Here, the hunter's boy could sit and see the wild cranes, geese, brants swim on the natural ponds and streams by the hundreds… These were all familiar to him in those days."[4]

Many Missouri gold hunters established mining camps and settlements along California streams, especially in the Sacramento area, enticing other

---

3 The *Hunnewell Graphic* ran the series as "R.M. Clark's Journey Across the Plains" with the subtitle "The Overland Route to California," consistently appearing on page 4, typeset as two columns.

4 Robert Clark, reflecting on his boyhood life in Marion County while en route to California in 1850.

Missourians to follow. As noted above, the young men (called *boys* in that era, regardless of age) who traveled from Northeast Missouri with the Clark brothers and whom Robert Clark frequently mentions in his memoir were Frank See, Mike Heckard, Carson Gatewood, and Henley Maddox. The appendix provides information about them and others from Missouri they met along the streams of California, including Bill Anderson, Bob Gosney, three Olivers: Wain, Stokes, and Boutwell, James Price, and a gentleman named Smoot. Others were Dave Davenport, Jim Hagar, two brothers of the name Fuson, and one fellow with the surname Brown. The appendix also includes a list of other Missourians Clark mentions as having a role in his memoir, from preparation to return.

For those who read these pages in appreciation of their ancestors from Northeastern Missouri, who may have ventured west or remained on Missouri ground (prayerful that the adventurers would return home safely if not also with new-found wealth), may your imaginations soar as you embrace the intelligence, courage, and character of these men and also of the women who managed homesteads, cultivated fields and cared for livestock while their enterprising men harvested dreams of adventure and financial security.

Regardless of the reason for holding this memoir, readers of Clark's recounting of his experiences seeking gold and the challenges of returning home safely can feel the thrill of adventure and expand their knowledge of this pivotal time in American history.

Marsha K. Clark
wife of James L. Clark, a great-grandson of Robert Mason Clark

Robert Mason Clark

R. M. Clark's
Journey Across the Plains

The Overland Route to California

THE DEPARTURE

During the month of January 1850, William Anderson, Frank See, [my] brother Sam and I would meet and consult the advisability of going to the gold region in quest of our fortunes. After some parleying and referring to Spotwood Williams' letters of that country, we determined to try to go. This Mr. Williams[5] was a resident of Marion County, a man of good judgment, very reliable, and crossed the plains in forty-nine. *Mr. Editor, I wish to say to you and those concerned, be patient with me and do not criticize my spelling or grammar, for my education is very much limited. I*

---

5 According to the 1860 US Census: "Spot S Williams" of South River Township, Marion County, Missouri, age 58, born in Virginia. A farmer. Real Estate is worth $10,250 [*purchased with gold money one might wonder*] and personal wealth of $6,049. Seven children. There are several ways this name is spelled in various records, including Spottswood. The Marion County records omit the second t yet does include the middle s. His gravestone (Sharpsburg Cemetery, Marion County) is carved *Spotswood.* A compilation of letters from Marion County, Missouri "49ers" during the Gold Rush period (Weant, 2004) includes information about Mr. Williams. On October 7, 1849, "S.S. Williams" (his middle name is Samuel) of Marion County sent a letter to his brother, A. G. Williams of Monroe County. This letter appeared on 24 January 1850 in the *Missouri Whig,* a newspaper in Palmyra, Missouri, a copy of which is provided in the Appendices. This letter gives many details about the mines, and it is most likely one of the letters that influenced the Clarks and friends to commence their 1850 journey. Interestingly, in another letter to the editor of the *Missouri Whig,* an unnamed letter writer reported from the gold fields that "Spottswood Williams, the brother-in-law of John Sharp has been absent some time, and I fear is sick, or he would have been here to wait on this brother-in-law." Time revealed that Sharp had died, but Spottswood returned as noted above in the US Census record, surviving to age 81.

never studied grammar or geography a day or learned the punctuation; therefore, you may often expect to find the cart before the horse.

Being determined to go, we set out to start in the spring by the overland route. There were oxen to buy, a wagon, and provisions to prepare and some duds to wear. So, the day was set to go out to buy oxen for our team. The day before we were to go to look after team, I counted up the cost and was sorry to learn that I was short of money to make up my portion of the outfit.[6] I expected to join Bill and Sam at Uncle Alex Anderson's early the next morning, so I went and found the boys and Uncle Alex planning for the trip. I remarked to the boys that they would have to count me out, for I did not have money to get me an outfit. Uncle Alex looked at me and said, "Bob do you want to go?"

"Yes, bad," I answered.

Then he said, "By the eternal you shall go. I will go with you and Bill today and buy some oxen for your team." So, we went and Uncle Alex bought three yoke of Uncle Billey Moss. We then drove the cattle to Uncle Alex's to feed and get [them] in good flesh for the trip.

Now we began to work and get ready in earnest. Sam and Bill went to Quincy [Illinois] and bought our wagon; and so now we had ox yokes to make, the wagon bed to partition off for our provision, and a score of other things to do. During this time, we met with Mike Heckard, Carson Gatewood, Henley Maddox.[7] They lived in North River near Palmyra and were fitting up for the trip. We proposed to go in company, which was accepted, and we entered into a leaguer[8] that we all were to have the

---

6 look after team: an expression meaning, to seek livestock for purchase; a team of oxen that would go with the young men on their journey.

7 Many Heckarts are listed as going to the California gold country in various sources. The spelling in those accounts is Heckart and sometimes Heckert or Heckard. Other Heckarts who went include brothers Adam and Florian (1850). Also, a Maddox: James of Ralls County. Several Andersons from Northeast Missouri also went west. The Andersons of Marion County—mainly Palmyra— were an educated and highly successful family of attorneys and, apparently, adventurous. (See appendix: Biographical Information)

8 Leaguer: a camp for defensive or offensive protection and unification, such as made by military units. Circling wagons—or schooners—is an example of a leaguer.

benefit and use, if need be, to the last ox until we got there. This now numbered seven of us all, with nine yoke of oxen and two horses to ride.

By this time our cattle were in a fine shape. We would hitch them up and drive them every few days. The last week in March, the weather was warm and balmy, so much so that we thought it would soon be time for us to pull out. We set April the 7th the day to start, which was Sunday. On Saturday, the day before, Heckard, Gatewood and Maddox drove up to Uncle Alex Anderson's. We had our wagon loaded and ready to start next morning. Sam and I staid [sic] at home that night and had an early breakfast. I did not eat much, for there was a lump in my throat. *Boys, when you come to bid farewell and leave the old parental roof, you then will understand what this means.*

We all met at Uncle Alex's, yoked, and hitched our teams. By this time, most all the men and boys in the neighborhood were there to see us start. Now it was time to say goodby, and it hurt some of us boys to say it to those good old mothers who had done so much for us. Quite a number of the men and boys went as far as New Market. We stopped there and rested. And just before starting again, Uncle Alex mounted his horse and rode out into the road in front of our wagons, rose up in his stirrups, and gave us a little speech of encouragement. As he turned to ride away, he looked at me and said, "Bob, crack your whip and go as long as you have an ox that can chew his cud."

We camped that night about two miles west of Warren,[9] near a branch close to where Dan Bell's store is now. That was fifty-three years ago, the seventh of last April. There were no improvements there then.

The second night, we camped on a creek west of Shelbyville.[10] That day, we fell in company with two wagons from Ralls County: one a horse and the other a mule team. There were seven young men in the

---

9 Warren was a village (est. 1854) in the southeast corner of today's Shelby County, previously a part of Marion County.

10 Shelbyville is in Shelby County, named after the first Governor of Kentucky, Isaac Shelby, who was a Revolutionary War soldier and leader on several levels in developing Kentucky. Interestingly, the Clark brothers' grandfather, Robert Vanschoiacke, served under General Shelby during the War of 1812. [Clark, R., 1905)

party: Dave Davenport, Jim Hagar, two Fuson boys, Tom J. Spalding, a young man named Brown, and one other I have forgotten. We concluded to go in company to St. Joe. By this time, the weather changed to cold rains and terrible, muddy roads. We were delayed making slow, short drives.

Our route passed through old Bloomington,[11] Macon County. We drove up in town one forenoon and stopped to rest. I sat down on a box to watch my team as I was driver that day. I was feeling blue. My mind was back to my old home with my old companions that I had left behind. The boys were scouting around town; whilst I sat there musing, a middle-aged gentlemen stepped up beside our wagon and printed on our wagon sheet, in big letters, these words: "Success to the enterprizing young men."[12] I looked up at the printing. I liked it. It did me good, and I felt better. It gave me new energy.[13]   Ever after, when I would get down in spirits or in hard places, I would look on the printing, and it would man me up. *Oh, we can never tell the good a little kind spoken word can do a disheartened boy.*

We drove on from Bloomington across the Chariton River and camped on the west side of the bottom near an old pioneer's cabin,

———✦———

11 Bloomington was the Macon County seat until 1863. It was northwest of Macon and 3.5 miles north of Bevier. The trail to Bloomington was first an Indian trail used by fur trappers, later becoming a route from Hannibal to St. Joseph. It was called the Bloomington Trail because its eponymous town was a crossroads in Macon County, near rivers providing an active thoroughfare for westward movement. (Sappington, Daviess County Historical Society)

12 On March 20, 1822, the *Missouri Republic* newspaper posted an ad from William H. Ashley for its St. Louis readers, announcing that 100 "Enterprising Young Men" were needed to work for the Rocky Mountain Fur Company, the young men keel-boating up the treacherous Missouri River to its source in Montana. The phrase must have been popular in that era of westward expansion. One account suggests this ad launched legendary explorer Jim Bridger westward (Vestal, S., p 8).

13 It was very common for wagon sheets to bear names of the states or lands of departure or slogans, such as "California or Bust" or "Patience and Perseverance"—Similarly to 20th century automobile bumper stickers. The Clark account of this uses a "z" in Enterprizing; therefore, it is retained here for the possibility that this truly may have been how the fellow traveler spelled it on the wagon canvas.

and bought feed of him for our stock. The weather continued cold and backward. That night, quite a shift of snow fell, and the ground froze some. The next morning, we bought a stalk field of our pioneer friend, consisting of six or seven acres and turned our stock on it. You remember, there were four wagons of us, eighteen head of oxen, six horses and four mules. We turned all our stock on the stalks. It did not look much like we were on our way to the gold regions that morning. That day we went turkey hunting.

This country all along here was thinly populated, especially the Chariton Bottom. Clad so heavy in her native forests, abounding in wild game and honey; the prairies adorned in summertime with native grass and set as with wild flowers. Here the wild deer loved to feed, sport and play. Here the hunter's boy could sit and see the wild cranes, geese, brants, swim on the natural ponds and streams by the hundreds. He could also hear the chatter of the timid squirrel in the forest; the cooing of the wild pigeon; the whirl of pheasant's wing, the call and gobble of the wild turkey, the drum of the prairie chicken, the whistle of the deer, the cry of the wild cat and the howl of the big black and gray wolf. These were all familiar to him in those days.

About the first of May, the weather got warmer and we thought we could venture to start for the plains, so we drove within a few miles of St. Joe and camped. The next day we walked to town. The streets were a perfect jam[14] with wagons and emigrants, with here and there on the corners a hand organ grinding away and the operator singing lustily, "Oh

---

14 To ensure there was enough grass for grazing, and to make sure the wagons crossed the mountains before snow season, April was the departure date from St. Joseph. One account in 1849 reported 6200 wagons waiting to cross the Missouri River by ferry, with wagons lined up "for miles," taking three weeks to reach the front of the queue, after which it took about four to five months to travel the 2,000 miles to reach California. (https://www. stjosephmo.gov/359/Gold-Rush)

California, it is the land for me. I am Bound for Sacramento, the gold dust for to see."[15]

That day, whilst we were in town, Mike Heckard fell in company with a Mr. Smoot, of Lewis County, Missouri. After becoming partially acquainted, Smoot proposed to Heckard that they organize a small train. Smoot and another man of his neighborhood had fit up two wagons and gave outfits to six young men for a certain share of what they make in a certain time, and this Smoot was to see after the other man's interests. The next day we drove up to where Smoot and some others had camped, and after looking over each other's teams and general outfit, we all agreed to go in and make up a train. We also accepted a wagon and four men that Smoot was acquainted with from Clark County and two from Indiana, which proved to be nice young men and a fine outfit. We now had a small train of seven wagons, twenty-five men, sixty-four head of oxen and seven head of horses.

We organized by electing Smoot captain and Heckard wagon master. We also had laid down rules in regard to standing guard and herding, and [we elected] not to travel on Sundays—only cases when we had not grass and water. We couldn't move on until we found it. Now we were about ready to cross over the river.

On the eighth day of May, we all drove up in town and bought feed and loaded all our wagons could hold. We drove to the ferry and ferried the river in the evening and drove out in the bottom and camped for the night. It was one month and one day since we left home. We parted with the Ralls Co. boys at St. Joe for the reason that horses, mules and cattle would not herd together; hence, we could not go in with the same train but met them further on.

---

15 Many songs from Stephen Foster and others were composed or had lyrics rephrased to relate to life during the Gold Rush era. Song historians Keith and Rusty McNeil collected "Moving West Songs," recorded as a collection available through WEM Records.

CROSSING THE MISSOURI RIVER AND THE PLAINS

As I said, we camped in the Missouri River bottom on the night of the 8th of May. Next morning, the 9th of May, we had a snow flurry. After breakfast, we yoked up and fell in line for the plains. That afternoon, we met quite a company of Indians. You ought to of seen the boys' eyes bulge out. They were sure Indians on their way to St. Joe trading. This was the first Indians we saw, and they were partially civilized.

About the third day we struck a strip of country freshly burned off. That night we gave the last of the feed to our teams. The country looked desolate and bare; no grass to be seen. The next morning, we pulled on not knowing how far the burned country extended. That afternoon we met some more Indians, and Heckard halted them. And, it so happened, there was one that could talk a little English. Heckard asked him if he could tell where we could find some grass. He said he could. And Heckard told him he could give him ten dollars if he would take us where our cattle could get some grass. The Indian agreed to do it. We pulled to the South, the Indian going before. In about four miles we came to a swale or slew with swamp-like grass. We stayed here three days, and our stock did very well.

By this time the weather was warm and nice, and [on] the fourth day we started again. Pulled for the trail and crossed over this burned strip the next day. We had it fine for some time, struck the great Platte Valley, and we had plenty of grass and water. Here we had some heavy storms, mostly after night. I remember one in particular. That evening was warm, and it was my night to stand guard. I was to go on at ten o'clock. Frank See and I slept in our wagon; Heckard and Bill Andersen and Sam in a tent; Gatewood and Maddox in their wagon. It being very warm, Frank and I lay down. We unbuttoned and rolled back the wagon sheet half-way. At ten o'clock, I was placed on guard. It was very dark and thundering in the West. The cloud came up slowly, but in the course of time the cloud shot up faster, and the lightning played fast. I wished the relief guard would come.

Pretty soon, the wind began to blow, and a few drops of rain [came] with it. This called to my mind the wagon sheet. I pulled for the wagon. I jumped up in front, pulled the sheet over but could not button it for the wind and hail. So, I drawed it down as tight as I could over the front gate, and sat there playing knucks with the hailstones, and Frank swinging onto the sheet next to the storm. In the meantime, Mike, Bill and Sam called to us to let them in for the wind had taken away their tent. We told them we could not, for the sheet was unbuttoned; and if we let go, the wind would strip off the sheet and our provisions get wet. So, they got under the wagon. Next morning, I do not think there was a tent standing in sight.

I will now try to tell how we arranged our wagons, horses, and cattle in camp. Heckard always selected the camping place. Sometimes in the afternoon he would ride on before, and look out a camping place, and meet us, and turn us out to camp. He was a splendid wagon master, for it seemed he never tired of the interest of the train. He would ride ahead to the camping place, take his stand, and the drivers would circle the teams and wagons around him. Then, at night, the wagons and teams would be in a circle. Every horse and ox had a picket, pin and rope; and if things looked squally, horses and cattle were brought inside the circle and picketed down.

Soon as we drove to camp, we unyoked. Herdsmen took charge of them and drove them to water and grass. At eight or nine o'clock, they were brought to camp and picketed inside the circle. In crossing streams, where there was danger of the water running up on our wagon beds, we would raise our beds in the standards as high as we dare and tie them there.

I do not remember much about the situation of old Fort Carney.[16] As I am writing this from memory, I will not try to describe it. *There are lots of things a man forgets in a lifetime but a few we never forget as long as life lasts.*

By this time, we boys were getting used to our mode of living and doing reasonably well, except one Dutch boy belonging to Smoot's wagon.

---

16 Fort Kearney in Nebraska. Clark's spelling hints to the pronunciation.

The Indians were a great terror to him. He became disheartened and terribly homesick and wanted to go home, for he said the Indians would kill us all. Heckard would talk to him and try to cheer him up. One morning he seemed dull and low spirited. Heckard asked him if he wanted to go home. He said yes; if Smoot would let him have his clothes, he would go.

Heckard spoke to Smoot about him and told him he might as well let him go. Smoot called the boy and asked him if he wanted to go home. He said, "I will, so if you will let me, and give me my clothes." Smoot told some of the boys to fix a pack and helped him off. So, he bade us all good by[e].

The fourth evening after he left we had pulled into camp and were un-yoking. I happened to look down the trail and saw a man walking and carrying a pack. I remarked to Bill, "I guess that fellow is going to pack through." As soon as Bill looked up he said, "Why, that is Hugh coming back!" And so it was. The men all stopped work and came to hear what Hugh had to say. Someone asked him why he came back. "Oh, I thought if I went on, the Indians would nail me, so I came back to die with you boys." Then we all hollowed [sic], "Hurrah for Hugh!" He seemed so glad that he could hardly contain himself, and ran around shaking hands with us. He went to work and made a first-rate hand in the train.

We had grass and water all the way up the Platte Valley. All the water was muddy-looking with sand in it; but to let it stand in a bucket, it would settle and clarify. The emigrants would dig a hole near the river and put a box or barrel in, and the water would seep in and be very fair.

We crossed the South Platte and went up the North.[17] The evening before, we camped as near as we could to get good grass. The next morning, [we] drove to crossing before breakfast, but when we got there, there were

---

17 Upon consulting with the managing director of the Oregon-California Trails Association, Travis Boley, it can be assumed the team followed the South Platte to west of what is now the village of Brule, Nebraska. There, they would cross over California Hill. After that, a train would drive slowly down the very steep decline of Windlass Hill to Ash Hollow. There are deep ruts visible at those places, supported today as part of the Oregon National Historic Trail by the National Park Service and Ash Hollow State Park.

two trains ahead of us, waiting to cross over. One was a large train with about three families belonging to it. There was a middle-aged gentleman superintending things. The man in charge started the big train first, then waited until they got quite a way out. Then [he] started the second one, then ours, leaving considerable space between. [He]charged us to be careful and not to let one team full up too close on another and stop; for, said he, "There is danger of your wagon going down, so you cannot pull out."

It happened to be my drive that morning, and my wagon to lead the train. The water was from knee deep to waist deep and pretty cool to tackle before breakfast, and it was said to be about a mile across. So, Bill and I concluded we would sit in the front of our wagon and drive. Our man gave the word to start, and from the way our wagon jostled, I was sure we were running over stone, and I remarked to Bill that it was rock instead of sand. But our team walked up too fast; we saw we would soon over-take the train before us. So, I jumped out in the water, which made me say, "Oh!" But I soon found why the wagon jostled. The water would whip the sand from under the wheels; hence, one would drop a little and then another. If I stood still a short time, I would be down almost knee-deep in sand.

We crossed without much ill convenience. Bill Anderson jumped out to help me hold back our team, and we both got wet and cold. Sam got out some dry clothes for Bill and I to change, and he took the whip to drive where we could get breakfast. About the time we got our wet clothes off ready to put on the dry, Bill said to me, in low voice nodding his head, "Bob, look there." I looked the way he indicated, and beheld there sat two nice-looking ladies in the front end of a wagon not more than ten steps away. As we had no place to run and hide, we stood our ground like good soldiers.

LARAMIE, THE BLACK HILLS,
KIT CARSON

We had fair sailing up the Platte until Laramie Fork. Here, the country became rough and broken. One afternoon a party of us boys concluded to take a hunt for game. So we strolled about a mile off from the trail, looking for sage hens; but instead, we came into a big town of prairie dogs. Those little creatures are in color of a brownish hue, about the size of a small squirrel. I guess they love company, for their town sometimes contains quite a number of houses. Neither do they have all in common but every pair or family is master of his own house. The town is not laid out in squares or blocks but in a circular form. The house consists of an entrance into the ground, sometimes straight, sometimes in a slanting position. The room is hollowed out beneath the surface and the dirt carried from around the entrance; hence, it formed a little mound a foot or so high.

On one entering a dog town, it seems the signal is given that you are coming, for you will see the landlords of the town at their doors on their mounds, sitting straight up on their haunches. And when you come in speaking distance, they speak with a chatter and fall back indoors. You see them no more on that visit. It is said a snake, an owl, and a dog will live together.

Now, the Black Hills began to loom up in the distance, and we drove on to the crossing of the Laramie Fork. When we came to the fork, we found a number of teams collected there. They were afraid to tackle it for the stream was considerably swollen. After Mike investigated, we concluded to try and cross. So, we blocked up our wagon beds and tied them fast. It being the day for captain Smoot's team to lead the train, he proposed to drive his team across himself.

Now, the Captain Smoot's team had a yoke of oxen in his team that he had worked at home on his farm, and he hitched them on the lead. "For," said he, "Logan will mind me." Logan was the lead oxen. He was a long, boney ox with great, big, wide horns. The captain had three yoke of small meat cattle and a big yoke at the wheels. The team looked rather comical with Logan in the lead.

The captain in the front end of the wagon, whip in hand, gave the word. Logan pulled in. When the team struck the current, the small cattle had to swim, and of course the swift water beat them downstream, forming a rainbow bend. Logan still kept wading, but the captain got somewhat excited, and he broke out like this: "Come on, Logan." But Logan made it all right, and we all crossed over without any loss. But we had the joke on the captain.

I do not remember how far it is from Laramie Fork to the fort. The train runs north of the fort. Here, we camped and rested a day. Brother Sam did the cooking for our mess all the way through, and he was a very economical cook. He had weighed and kept account of all the provisions we had consumed up to this time. At breakfast that morning, he said, "Boys, I have made a fair estimate of our provisions, and I find we will lack one-hundred pounds of flour to carry us through. I also hear that there is flour to sell at the fort. Now will you all chip in and buy a hundred pounds more?" We said we would.

After breakfast, brother Sam and Mike Heckard went to the fort, and Sam bought the flour. It cost sixteen dollars a hundred, but it was luck that we got it. I was not at the fort, for I was on herd that day. So, I cannot tell much about it. I think there were about one company of soldiers there, and there were some tame buffalo and a small field in cultivation. This was the last improvement I saw on the plains.

Now for the Black Hills, near here we lost an ox.[18] He got to an alkali pool and drank so much that he became disabled and could not keep up with the train. Those Black Hills proved to be hard on us and

---

18 The travelers are on the plain of Southeast Wyoming. Clark is describing the Laramie Mountain Range. In the era of the pioneers, these mountains were called the Black Hills. These are not to be confused with the Black Hills known today in Southwest South Dakota and Northeast Wyoming. (Oregon Trail Mileposts – End of the Oregon Trail, August 2024. historicoregoncity.org)

our teams. The trail was rough and gritty, which rasped the oxen's hooves and made them tender and sore. The alkali dust and grit hurt our eyes so much that we had to wear goggles.

One day, we stopped for dinner, and word came to us that Kit Carson was just around the bend from us, so away we went to see The Grizzly. The word kept going, and the emigrants kept coming until there was quite a crowd collected. When we got around, sure enough there were six or seven government wagons loaded with buffalo hides. And a little way off, we saw a man lying on a buffalo rug. This was Kit Carson. As we approached, he raised up and rested his hand on his elbow. Some of the emigrants asked him several questions, but he did not seem very talkative. But, [he] said something about our road and thought best for us to go by Subletts Cutoff[19] and spoke of several tribes of Indians that we would have to pass through and their characteristics. I will never forget what he said concerning the Pawnee tribe. He said, "Shoot every one on sight and never trust one." As he lay there, he did not seem to me to be a very large or tall man, but he was a rough, stout-looking fellow. Neither did he shrink to look him in the eye. He was on his way to St. Joe.

We were now in the midst of a wild, desolate-looking country—or was then. All along there, a man never knew where he was, for one place looks just like every other place. I thought of Frank See's description of that country. One day, he was scouting around and did not get in until

---

19 The cutoff, first traveled in 1844, would bypass a meandering 85-mile loop of trail that took emigrants past Fort Bridger in what is now southwest Wyoming. However, this detour was rugged, with no shade or drinkable water. Stopping was frequent and did not save time. The cutoff was marked by abandoned wagons and carcasses of animals. By taking the cutoff, which was twenty-five miles north of Fort Bridger, travelers would bypass the trading post established by mountain man Jim Bridger. Bridger was not pleased, so he sent a partner to South Pass to encourage travelers to take the old route. Regarding Mr. Sublette: "[He] was a fur trader and "mountain man" who would later retire in St. Louis, building a substantial estate east of S. Hampton & Manchester Road one-half mile south of Forest Park in St. Louis, near what was a Sulphur Spring; the nearby street, Sulphur, marks the site. Sublette Street continues to run north and southeast of the old estate, none of which remains today." (Blackwood, G., Life on the Oregon Trail. Lucent Books, 1999. p.33; Vestal, Jim Bridger, p 164)

we had hitched up for the afternoon drive. I was putting away pans and cups and cold vituals[20] when Frank came riding up and called out, "Bob, have you anything for me to eat?" I answered him by saying, "Where have you been, lost?"

"No, Bob; I've been prospecting this country."

"Well, what conclusion have you made?"

"God almighty never made this country. He made the States and all back where we lived, but not this country. You know, the Devil always tries to imitate God the Almighty. When God got through making the States, the Devil thought he could do something, so he turned in and made all this country. That's why it is so rough."

Along here, the ox teams began to close up on the horse and mule teams, and at nine o'clock in the morning, there was a train of wagons as far as the eye could see, east or west. In the mountainous country, we boys had it pretty hard, for we often had trouble to find grass for our stock. We would often leave the trail three or four miles to get grass and water, and to make us feel worse, the cholera was creeping up on us. One day, on Saturday, we saw three corpses a little way off the trail. You remember I said one of our rules was to lay by on the Sabbath unless circumstances would not permit. On Sunday morning, after we passed those corpses, the train came together in council to know the feelings of the train, whether we wished to stay or try and keep ahead of the cholera. After consulting the captain, [we] put it to a vote whether to go or stay. All voted to go except two wagons: those Indiana boys, and we could not persuade them to go. So, we drove on and left them. They were nice young men. The cholera overtook them, and three of the seven died.

Our wagon master adopted this plan to put us farther ahead. We would start one hour sooner of a morning and travel one hour later of evening than usual, for there was no such thing as whipping around trains. If a train had pulled out of the trail, the other trains would pull up and block him out until noon or night.

We had comparatively little trouble with the Indians. They tried to

---

20 the word *victuals*, meaning food; colloquial pronunciation: "vittles"

stampede our stock one night. We camped on a creek called Thompson's Fork. It so happened we had our stock all picketed down. I had just been released off guard when I heard yelling and bells jingling, coming down the valley. Our guards ran down in front of our wagons the way they were coming. Pretty soon we could see them coming. When they came near enough, the guards fired and the Indians sheared off. None of our stock broke loose. The way they do to stampede stock is to bell the ponies they ride, run into a bunch of stock, give the Indian yell, and let their bells all loose. Then, the stock becomes frightened and run, and fall in front with their ponies, and run through other herds. The frightened stock follow the ponies. I think there were as many as one hundred head in the stampede that night.

As soon as the stampede passed us, Captain Smoot ordered seven men to mount horses (for those were all the horses we had) and follow. About the time the men were ready to start, about twenty men came galloping up and our men fell in with them. After running about two miles, they passed all the stock—or they thought they had. The Indians turned into a canyon and made for the mountains. Our men circled the cattle and horses, and succeeded in bringing them in. But the next morning, there were twenty horses and mules gone. We staid until noon but had no word of them so we left and never heard whether they ever found them or not.

One day before the stampede, we stopped for noon, and the second train before us was a large train containing two or three families. Whilst there, a squad of ten Indians came up. Some of them appeared to be drinking. One of them approached a wagon where a lady was sitting in the front end. The woman screamed and called for help. Now, this lady's husband was taking with him a black man, and he, being a little way off, heard his mistress' call. He ran, and as he ran, he picked up his ox whip and ran in between the Indian and the wagon. But the Indian dodged around the negro and jumped upon the wagon tongue, making for the woman. The negro turned the big end of his ox goad[21] and gave him one lick on the head, which killed him dead. As soon as the white men saw what the negro had done, they slipped him into another wagon and hid him. The Indians came up and appeared very mad and demanded the black man. But

---

21 A goad is a pointed, long tool to spur or guide livestock

the whites kept him concealed. After prowling around a while, they loaded the dead Indian on a pony and carried him away. The whites concluded in all probability the Indians would return with help, so they collected the men of four trains and waited. In about two hours the Indians came back with twenty-five more and gave the whites to understand that if they would give up the black man to them, they would go off [peacefully]. But they would not give up the black man to them, but kept him closely hid and threatened to shoot the Indians if they did not leave right away. So, they kept the Indians off and would not let them come near. We moved on that evening and kept out strong guards several nights.

THE ROCKS

I went to see the Chimney Rock. It is situated south of the emigrant trail, and composed of a soft, dark-colored rock. I have forgotten how tall they claimed it to be. The base is covered with names and dates cut in the rock as high up the stem as they could climb. I was also at the Steamboat Spring, Soda Spring, Castle Rock and Court House Rock.[22]

The Steamboat Spring was a considerable curiosity to me. The water seems to have a sediment in it, which I have no doubt has been forming for ages. This cement has formed around the vein, I will say six feet across and about two feet high, closing up so close on the vein as to shut out the air. This gives it a kind of suction, which gives it a gushing of a jug; and by turning it upside down, you know how the water will gush out with a sound, hence the name Steamboat.

We camped near the Soda Springs and at the Hot Springs. I have heard said the water could poach an egg, but I think you would wait a long time for your poached egg. We camped near a branch of water one cool night. The next morning, the warm steam arose from the warm water, warm enough for a nice bath.

As some people may think the emigrants had a fine time shooting game, I will give a little of our experience on the game question. There was but one bunch of about thirty buffaloes ever in sight of our train. We saw numbers of antelopes; but if you had to shoot one to get steak

---

22 These are located on the south side of the North Platte River on the Nebraska panhandle. Visiting these geographic marvels occurred before the events described on the previous pages, when they were in Wyoming.

for breakfast, I fear your breakfast would be quite late. They are very wild, fleet cunning animals, and they come as near to flying as any footed animal that I ever saw. The most game that we got on the plains were sage hens.

Well, I must get to my train again for it is nearing the American Desert now. Teams are giving out, trains are going to pieces. Sometimes, men quarrel and divide teams. I heard of one mess that cut their wagon bed in two, and each party took two wheels. And there, by the side of the trail, stood the Ralls County boys' wagons and harness laying on the ground. Their horses gave out, and they packed what they could on their mules. *Little did I then think that I would live to know that the [train] cars would pass through that country daily, or that my children would inhabit it, for the general opinion with us then was that it was fit for nothing— only the Indian, buffalo and wild animals.*[23]

Our train camped as near to the desert as we could in order to get sufficient grass for our stock and rested a day. It seems like we started on the desert in the morning, traveled that day and night; and next day, about one o'clock, we came to Green River. The desert is sixty miles across, and here we had to ferry the river. We ferried the wagons over and swam the cattle. This stream is swift and dangerous to swim in as a number of persons have been drowned there. I did not see much of the country here for several days as I had a severe attack of cholera morbus[24] and was unable to drive or be on duty for several days.

After crossing the river, the train moved a short distance, and we camped and rested our teams. Here the boys spent the Fourth of July. Having found a keg of powder on the road a few days before, they kept it to celebrate with. They also tapped a keg of brandy and had a jolly time bombarding and shooting at marks. *Boys, excuse me for telling on you.*

Here we wound around the foothills of mountains on our left. And

---

23 See appendix Clark Families for a listing of Robert Mason Clark's and wife Sarah Jane (Gosney)'s children. Son James David Clark (m. Louisa Hagar 1878, Ralls County, MO) moved to Buffalo, Wyoming between 1900 and 1910, and died there in 1933.

24 Gastroenteritis (diarrhea, vomiting, cramps) was caused frequently by eating excessive amounts of decomposing buffalo meat. These are symptoms similar to the deadly cholera, but not the same.

way up on the mountain range, it seemed like there were caves in those cliffs. It seemed, also, like you could see doors in the white rock, and they were arranged in a straight line as if by art. All along through here were grand sceneries of nature.

One day, we came to a place off to the right of the trail that might be called a canyon but it was called the Devil's Pass.[25] So a parcel of boys concluded to go through it, and as I was off of driving I went along. There was a considerable streak of water that seeped through it. When we got to the entrance, we could pass by, being careful between the stream and the perpendicular wall of rock. I do not know how high it was from the bed of the creek to the top of the wall, but it seemed to me to be two hundred feet or more. There were numbers of swallows in there, raising their young.

After passing up some distance, our footway gave out, the water coming up with such force against the wall that made it splash and foam. Seeing we could go no further that way, we found some steps like crevices in the wall; and on examining, we could distinguish some foot marks. So after climbing and resting, we finally got on top. After going about fifty yards on top, we came to where we had to go down again. I believe going down was as bad as going up, for there were only little steps or benches that we could stop on and rest a little.

After we got down, we walked out on a small valley. We traveled Sublette's Cutoff. Consequently, we did not see the Mormon city or the great Salt Lake.

Miles and Bennett of St. Louis fit up a mule train that season for the purpose of taking passengers across the plains for a stipulated amount. I

------

25 There are several Devil's Gate rock formations and Devil's Pass in Nevada, California, Wyoming, and elsewhere. Here, we can assume Clark describes a pass in Wyoming, near Independence Rock near Sweetwater River. These are in south central Wyoming, west of Ft. Laramie. Independence Rock is recorded as "130 feet high, 1,900 feet long, 850 feet wide" [wyohistory.org; National Park Service]. The name "Independence Rock" derives from the time in July that plains travelers would arrive after departing from the Missouri gateway, and would camp there to celebrate the nation's declaration of independence–as noted in the paragraph above.

have forgotten how many there were in the train, but a good-sized train. They passed us on the Platte River, and along here, between Green River and the Humbolt, their train went down, and they packed what they could. I think their mules were too young for the trip and probably drove too hard. I did not know how they came out, but understood the company lost money. The company consisted of Pete, Mike Wiles and Bennett. At one time this Pete Miles lived in Monroe County.

One Sunday, we camped near the Courthouse Rock. Whilst at dinner, brother Sam remarked that he had no wood to cook supper with. I answered I would get on the mare and go to yonder cedar bluff, which seemed not to be far, and get some dry cedar. So, I started about two o'clock, and when I got there, things had a different appearance from what they had from camp. I rode up to the edge of the cedars, got down, hitched my mare, and walked in amongst the trees to get the dry limbs.

Then quite a number of dirty-looking or brownish colored birds met me. They did not fight me, nor did they seem to be afraid, but would jump down on the limbs over my head, ruffle up their feathers and squall at me. It seemed to me they were trying to find out what kind of being I was, and I almost concluded that I was the first white man that had ever been to that cedar bluff. Well, I got my bundle of sticks, tied them up as quick as I could, and hurried away, for the queer actions of the birds made me feel lonely, and it was actually five o'clock when I got to camp. I do not think I was ever so badly deceived in distance anywhere on the plains or in mountains as here.

THE HUMBOLT RIVER

We were pulling on towards the head of the Humbolt River, or St. Mary's as it was once called.[26] The boys, as well as teams, were feeling worn and tired out. Grass was getting scarce, provision getting short with a great many, and with none to buy, we were all making a life struggle, as it were, to get down the river and cross the desert. For indeed, we had a long, wearisome, hard pull ahead of us; and with that anxiety, the whole emigration wished to be over the desert.

We were now passing deserted wagon after wagon, pile after pile of as good harness (as good as the shops could turn out), ox yokes and chains—all left by the wayside. I had seen fine guns with the locks off, barrels bent over wagon wheels, and instances where they threw away all but one suit of clothes.

When we came to the Humbolt, good old Mike Heckard said, "Boys, we must be as good to our oxen as we can if we have to work almost night and day to save them through this hard drive." And we did work almost night and day. We traveled through a great deal of sand going down this river, with barren sandy strips or small deserts five, even fifteen miles across. Consequently, after ten o'clock. the sun shining on the sand made the afternoon very warm, so we adopted the plan of making all of our heavy drives after night and early mornings. And we had to labor under

---

26 This river runs across the northern region of Nevada, parallel with Interstate 80 and the trail that brought emigrants into California gold Country. The area between Fernley and where route 95 meets Interstate 80 is known as the Forty Mile Dessert, between the Humboldt River and the Carson River, from the Humboldt Sink and Humboldt Bar.

the difficulty of using bad water, for we had to use the river water, which was dirty with sand and tinctured considerably with alkali. Drinking this weakened both man and beast.

As feed was scarce, we boys would take advantage of every opportunity that presented to get buck, pike or duke a few mouthfuls of something to eat. There were small patches of young willow growing near the river on the opposite side from us, and we boys would swim over, cut a bunch, and bring it back to the oxen. As we did the most of our travel down this river after night—and in daytime spent a considerable portion of the time seeing after the cattle and looking for grass—we did not get over portion of sleep. At times we would get very sleepy and tired.

Around midnight one night as we were crossing a ten- or twelve-mile strip of sand, I was relieved from driving and concluded to walk on ahead of the train. In a short time, I became so sleepy and thought I would walk slow until the train came up, so I could get in the wagon for a little sleep. The last I knew, I heard the boys talking to their teams. I never knew how I got down, but I got down all the same. Next morning, I woke up by the sun shining in my face. I could not realize for a while where I was or how I came there. But when I got on my feet and looked around, it all came plain. The next thing was which way should I go. So, looking away off I saw a train coming towards me, so I took the way the train was coming. When I got over to the boys, they had the laugh on me and were fixing to go back to look after me.

I only had four or five miles to walk, for they had crossed over and come to a little grass. There was but little danger of Indians here. I had not seen [a single] Indian on the Humbolt River. The trail changed from side to side and back and forth several times, so we crossed the river several times. At last, one evening, just before camping time, we came to the last crossing, the crossing that led out to Humbolt Meadows. The meadows were not immediately on our route, but the emigrants went there to rest up and to cut grass and make hay to feed their teams whilst crossing the desert.

As I said, we came to the last crossing, and as it was a bad crossing, the delay caused a great throng. Seeing that our train could not get over that evening, Mike ordered us to unhitch, take the herd tent and six herdsmen, and go back with the cattle about four miles to a certain bend, a horseshoe bend in the area. So, we went and found the place all right, and some nice grass. The entrance into this bend was a narrow strip. So we put the oxen in the bend and pitched the tent on this narrow strip.

Now, everything looked secure. At eight o'clock we concluded to put on only one guard so we could get as much rest as possible. The first guard went on duty with the understanding that at the end of two hours to come to the tent and wake up the next man. At the expiration of the time the guard came and woke up his man and reported all things quiet, and said he did not think it worthwhile to keep out a guard, that the oxen were all lying down resting. So we all got laid down and went to sleep. Next morning, when we went after the cattle, there was one ox missing, and we could not find him. Bill Anderson inquired of some men who said they saw some men across the river from our cattle a jurking[27] beef to take them over the desert, and from the description we supposed it to be our ox and looked no further. We yoked up and took the teams to the wagons. The boys hitched the teams to the wagons and crossed over while we herdsmen ate our breakfast then drove out to the meadows. We had lost one yoke of oxen from our team, leaving only three oxen to take us over the desert.

The sweet meadow looked nice and green only in places. The grass was considerably grazed off and tramped down. We drove around to the east where the grass was nice and pretty. Here we camped and turned our cattle to graze. This is where the Humbolt sinks and makes the meadow. The earth seemed to be full of crevices or caverns, and when the water comes to one of these crevices—not being large enough to receive all the water—it goes on to the next, and next, and so on until it spread over a considerable piece of land, irrigating the ground and thus causing the grass and vegetation to grow. *Oh, the wonderful mysteries of nature.* I do not know how large the meadow is.

---

27 Referring to drying beef, or creating beef jerky.

CROSSING THE DESERT

The second day after coming to the meadow, we began to prepare to cross the desert. We cut grass and let it cure in the sun and made hay to take on the desert for our cattle. We also took all our provision and clothes from our wagon and put them in Heckard's wagon and loaded our wagon with hay and water. With the train now ready, each man filled his canteen with water, and at two o'clock in the afternoon, we struck the desert. We traveled until eight o'clock when Mike called a halt. He turned us out of the trail, and we unhitched, gave our teams some hay and water, ate some supper, and rested one hour. As I said, we had only three yoke of oxen now. We loaded our wagon team when Mike called a halt; our team was considerably jaded, but after feeding and watering, our load was lighter. After resting one hour, we hitched and drove on.

Now we began to overtake lots of broken-down stock and wagon after wagon standing by the trail on the sand. The owners would gather up such as they could carry and go on. At midnight, Mike called another halt, so we stopped, unhitched, gave the most of our hay and water to the oxen, and rested again. When we went to hitch our team to start again, I found one of our team so stiff and tired that he was not able to go in the team. We hitched one yoke of Heckard's with ours, led the odd ox behind the wagon, and told Frank See to take the mare on through to water. Brother Sam said he would try and bring the broke down ox on, so he filled his canteen and waited for the ox to rest, leaving Bill and I to take care of the team.

At daylight, we stopped again, gave the last of our feed and water to the oxen, made some coffee and had a little breakfast, and pulled out on our last drive. At nine o'clock, the sand was getting hot, and all the boys were gone but the driver. Heckard had gone on to save his horse. Bill Anderson and Henley Maddox had left, and as Gatewood and I were on drive, we had to stay from nine to ten o'clock.

We were making short drives as the teams would pull up a quarter to a half a mile and stop. The sun and sand were so hot that someone proposed to leave the wagons and come and get them when the sun got low; but no one felt willing to sit there all day and watch the provision. Whilst we thus parlayed, our cattle raised their heads and stood a minute, like sniffing the air, and then moved up without stopping on their own accord the rest of the way. We were near two miles away when we claimed they scented the water, so we pulled over and came to a beautiful stream called Sweet Water, or that is what the emigrants called it, at about eleven o'clock.[28] Sam did not get in until near one o'clock, but he had to leave the ox about six miles back on the desert. Sam said the ox was getting weak, and as he was passing a deserted wagon near the trail, the ox struck the shade of the wagon and dropped down; Sam could not get him up any more.

The water in Sam's canteen had given out and he was becoming very thirsty. Just beyond the desert the Mormons kept a trading post. Also two men hauled water on the desert to sell to the immigrants. As Sam came in, he met those men and gave them twenty-five cents for a drink. Bill Anderson and I thought of going after night to try to bring the ox in, but we felt so tired that we concluded to wait until early in the morning. That evening—a while before sunset—I went on herd, and feeling weary, I sat down on a knoll. My eye scanned the valley. I could see a pure, bright stream of water angling its way through the valley away off there in front of me. On the foothills were splendid forests of stately pines towering the sky. The sun was sinking to rest behind the summit of the Sierra Nevada mountains, and the light streak that shot up from the sun made all look

---

28 It appears Clark is describing several events in his memoir that don't flow in a continual westward path. Several states have waterways named Sweetwater. Sweetwater River Valley is near Independence Rock in Wyoming and was an important place to stop along the trail west. In the above paragraph, we assume Clark is describing the Sweetwater Mountains at the border of Mono County in California and Lyon County in Nevada.

lovely, beginning to twinkle. Oh, it was a beautiful sight! Whilst I thus set meditating and wandering, those lines of my favorite boyhood piece of poetry came floating to my mind.

The spacious firmament on high, with all the blue ethereal sky,
And spangled heavens a shining. From the original proclaim.
The unwearied sun from day to day Doth his creator's power display,
And published to every land. The work of an Almighty hand.
Soon as the evening shade prevails. The moon takes up the wondrous tale.
And nightly to the listening earth Repeats the story of her birth.
While all the stars around her burn. And all the planets in their turn
Confirm the tidings as they roll. And spread the truth from pole to pole[29]
In reason, here they all rejoice. And utter forth a glorious voice,
Forever singing as they shine. The hand that made them is Divine.[30]

The cut fires along the valley now began to throw out their light and the emigrants going from one to another shaking hands and congratulating one another, for we all felt as though we could now get through, as we could get some provisions, though at exorbitant prices. I have seen flour sell for one dollar a pint.

That night was the last time I saw the Ralls County boys except Dave Davenport and Jim Hagar. The next morning, Bill Anderson and I started at the peep of day after our broken down ox. We took a bunch of grass and each a canteen of water. When we got to the desert, we saw the poor horses, mules, and oxen wandering over the barren sand,

------

29 Lines of the poem omitted between pole and in reason are: *"What though in solemn silence all ~Move round the dark terrestrial ball? ~What though no real voice nor sound ~ Amid the radiant orbs be found?"* The poem, "Ode" (to the glory of God) or Divine Ode was written by British man of letters Joseph Addison, appearing August 1712 in *The Spectator* (a magazine he co-founded), following an essay he composed about man's relationship with a Creator. The poem serves as lyrics for a hymn used in many Christian worship hymnals, sung frequently to Franz Haydn's Chorus No. 14 "The heavens are telling" from Haydn's oratorio, The Creation, first performed in 1799.

30 Hymn paraphrased from Psalm 19:1-6

horses neighing, oxen lowing. Some were dead, others not able to walk, and wagons, harness, chains and ox yokes lying here and there.

When we got out far enough we easily recognized the wagon where Sam left the ox, for he described it so minutely that we could not mistake it. But there was no ox there. In all probability, it had wandered away during the night, so we sat down in the shade of the wagon to rest. There were no trains in sight yet, it being too early in the morning for them to get that far on the last drive. Whilst we sat there, we noticed a man coming from the west. When he came where we were, he said that he was looking for a broken down oxen that he left there the day before. Bill remarked that we had one there and that we would keep him company. In case we found them, we could help one another. Whilst there, we noticed the main part of the stock were beating a southeast direction, so we concluded to follow in that direction. After going some three or four miles, we came to a small lake. The thirsty stock would rush to it, plunge in and sup a mouthful but could not swallow it [because] it was so salty. They would open their mouths and let it run out. Poor things. It looked hard after striving so hard to get there.

I do not know how many acres this lake contained, maybe a hundred and maybe not over half of that. We did not walk around it. There were no high banks, but it sloped gradually in some shells and rocks at the water's edge. From the rippling of the water on the rocks and the action of the sun and air, there was created salt on the rock. While sitting, talking, and wondering, we noticed a ripple on the water every few minutes, spoke of it, and watched. As near as we could guess, it came every ten or fifteen minutes, and it seemed to us that we heard a sound just like the whizzing sound of a flock of birds' wings in the air. There was no grass and but very little vegetation here.

As our time was passing, we started back, angling towards the trail passing a bunch of straggling stock here and there. On our way back to the trail, our man found one of his oxen, so we managed to get him along slowly. We got to the trading post a little before sunset. Mick Heckard had said to Bill and I that morning that it might be that they would move farther down the valley that day in order to get the better grass. When we came to where we could see where we were camped, low and behold, they had gone. Our man said his train had gone.

Those fellows at the post would give a little something for broken down stock. The owner of the ox said, "It is no use trying to overtake the train with this ox, so I will try and sell him." We managed to get the ox around, and our man called out the trader and asked what he would give for the ox. The trader gave him ten dollars and asked if he did not wish to buy some provision. He wanted to know if he had anything to eat. The trader said they had pies and cake. The man said to us, "Come boys, we will eat up the ox." Then we went into the trader's shop, and he asked the man what he would have. "I will take that ten dollars all in pies," said our man. "All right," remarked salesman. He counted him five pies made of dried apples, the crust as thin as could be made and the fruit as thin in proportion. I believe I could have eaten it all.

After eating our pies and taking a drink of water, we walked on; and to relief, we did not have to walk very far until Bill and I caught up with our train. The man walked on, and that is the last I ever heard of him. These men at the trading post, Mormons they were said to be, collected a big drove of stock one way and another: some they bought, some picked up, and others broke down. They would drive them on the Carson Valley and herd them until just time to cross the mountain before snow shut them in. Then they drove to Sacramento and auctioneered them off. I heard the auction lasted two weeks.

Frank See succeeded in getting our mare over the desert, but she got too much water and got stiff and weak. The next morning, after Bill and I came from the desert, the boys concluded that the mare would do us no more good, so they gave her to me. I took her up to the trading post and sold her for ten dollars—but did not eat pies. Here, our train parted as Heckard wanted to rest our teams before starting over the mountains, and the other boys were anxious to go on. So, we bade each other goodbye. Frank See concluded that he wanted to go on, so we got out what provision he could carry with some boys that packed through.

I can say that, in honor of the boys, we all parted good friends and crossed the plains with as little wrangling as any train. There were just six of us boys that left Uncle Alex Anderson's of Old Marion on that memorable morning of April 7th, 1850.

We moved farther down on the Carson Valley and camped and rested six days. We had fine pasture here. Our oxen gave us no trouble.

They had good pure water to drink and the best of grass to eat. After enjoying a six-days rest beneath the shade of the splendid pine forests near the foothills, with here and there a little rivulet of bright sparkling water trickling down the foothills, we arranged to climb the Sierra Nevada Mountains.

SIERRA NEVADA MOUNTAINS

We had our provision and goods in Heckards wagon when we crossed the desert. We let them remain there. We ran our wagon in the Carson River and left her afloat, hitched seven yoke of oxen to the Heckard wagon, and pulled for Old Sierri. Then we came to the ascent of the mountain. We rested and then started up. After going up a while, we came to muddy water running in the wagon ruts then to slush and snow. We felt cool and chilly and put on some more clothing. Next, we came to snow banks, and before we reached the summit, we had our overcoats on.

The descent was rough and rocky. We had to keep a sharp lookout to keep from turning the wagon over. That night we camped on a piece of table land with a mountain peak on both sides. There was a considerable bunch of grass growing here; although, I guess, the altitude is pretty high, as we had a big frost that night and a thin skim of ice froze over a bucket of water sitting out. The next day, we made slow progress as the way was very rough. We passed an awful rough canyon with hardly [any] room to get around. There were great big boulders, then steep sidling places. The boys fixed some ropes on the sides to hold to and to keep the wagon from turning over. After a few more days of travel, the trail got more smooth, and we soon made better time.

Now we began to keep a pretty sharp lookout, for we had heard that when we came to the oak timber we would be in the gold region. When we saw the oak trees, you would have laughed to see how our eyes shot around at each other as though we were afraid that some other fellow might get the first piece of gold that the wagon wheel might throw out.

WEAVERVILLE

As we were now near the end of our journey, we were feeling pretty good. At about one o'clock on the evening of August 30th, we drove into the mining town called Weaverville, near the McCosmey River.[31] The first fellow that I met that I knew was Frank See. He was glad to see me. He made it with his pack all right and made good time. After looking around town a while, we drove down near the river and unyoked our team for the last time—it being four months and twenty-three days from the time we left home.

Heckard had exceptional good luck with their team, for they took in all their oxen and horses. We lost three oxen and our mare. In the course of two or three days we made sale of all of our cattle, and Mike also sold their horse. We got sixty-dollars a yoke, or in other words, thirty dollars per head all around and divided the money proportionally.

After Frank See got his money, he went with some acquaintances.

---

31 This is in El Dorado, not Trinity County, California, which also has a Gold Rush town called Weaverville. Clark's Weaverville was Weberville (also Webberville), but the pronunciation was frequently Weaverville, presumably a result of Hispanic presence (soft middle b). Weberville is now part of Placerville, El Dorado County. Named for Captain Charles Weber, founder of Stockton, California, this river held the first gold mining camp in the area. Weber Creek is a stream that empties into the American River about halfway between the town of Coloma and Mormon Island. It was an area with a rich gold vein, appearing in the gravel bars and the creek bed. The 1850 census shows 906 inhabitants in Weaverville (net of duplicate names during the time of census as miners traveled around from site to site; the original census recorded 966 inhabitants in the settlement). See Bibliography sources.

We six kept together, that is Mike Heckard, Carson Gatewood, Henley Maddox, Sam Clark, Bill Anderson, and myself.

After selling our teams and resting a few days, we purchased us some mining tools: a rocker to wash the gold from the clay and gravel, two picks, two shovels, one pan, and two buckets. I have forgotten how much our tools cost, but I assure you it was enough. I have given one ounce of gold for a shovel.

The rocker was a small concern made mostly of pine lumber built on rockers and resembled the old-styled baby cradle. It took one man to operate the cradle and two to dig dirt and carry to the cradle. So, Bill, Sam and I worked pardners. Mike, Henley and Carson ran their outfit. I must give you my first days experience in mining, not that you will learn anything, but for fun.

The morning after we bought our tools, Bill said to me, "Bob, let's go prospecting today." I said alright. Bill was a big stout fellow, and he said he would carry the rocker and pick while I could carry the shovel, pan, and bucket. So, we lashed the rocker on Bill's back, shouldered up the tools, and away we went to the river.

The river was very low, barely running when we came to it. There was a great many fellows there, walking over the riffles, peaking in the crevices, and picking up rock looking for gold. They seemed much disappointed and had but little to say, but [the men] looked at Bill with his rocker on his back rather inquiringly. Bill said to me in a low tone, "Bob, let's go on where there isn't so many." We did not wish to learn those fellows anything about getting gold, so we trudged on down the creek, or river as it was called, until we passed them all and came to a dry gulch or ravine where the water in time had cut a considerable ditch. Bill stopped and looked around and said, "I wonder if here would not be a good place to try?" I said I thought it would.

We took down the rocker, and as there was a good hole of water close by. Bill said, "You set the rocker and wash, and I will dig and carry dirt." The inside of a rocker is constructed something like a wheat fan. The bottom plank is nailed fast to two rockers. Then you put on your back end plank. Then, a three-inch strip in front is nailed on the end of the bottom plank. Another strip two and one-half inches wide, about one foot back on the bottom board. Another strip one and one-half inches on the back of the second one. Have them extend clear across the bottom. Nail all fast to the bottom. Put on your side boards. Nail them into the edge of your bottom and to your back end board. Cut a front end board and leave a space open of two or three inches between it and the first bar so the mud and water can run off. Back of those bars is where the gold will lodge.

Now make an apron of two strips of lumber lacking two or three inches of being as long as your rocker. Get a piece of canvas, stretch it tight, and nail it to those strips with small nails. Have it the same width as your rocker. Put some strips on the inner side of the rocker for your apron to rest on. Place them so the apron will be in a slanting position, dropping near the bottom at the far end. Make a box eighteen inches square, and get a piece of sheet iron or zinc the same dimensions. Punch it full of one-half-inch holes. Nail it on the open end of your box. This is your hopper and riddle. Nail a handhold on the hopper. Then, nail cleats on the rocker to hold the hopper in place.

I set my rocker in a slanting position as near to the way as I had been instructed. Bill had some dirt ready, and I threw a bucketful in the hopper and began to dip and pour water with one hand and to rock with the other, taking the hopper off and emptying out the rocks that were too large to go through the riddle. Bill and I were whooping things. I lifted off the hopper to empty out the loose rock when I saw a piece of gold caught fast in one of the holes in the riddle.

I caught it, and holding it up in my fingers, I called to Bill, "I've got it." Bill came running and took it from my fingers, and laid it in his hand, and both stood admiring it. When Bill thought of the rocker he said, "God, what's in the rocker?" We both jumped at the rocker. I jerked out the apron and scratched down in the sand and back of the bars but found no gold. We got the pan, cleaned out the rocker, panned out the rocker and panned out the sand and gravel as best we could but did not get a color. We fixed up and went to work again and washed about twenty buckets more and cleaned up again but found no color. So we packed up and struck for camp. We got there and showed our gold to the boys. Then, we went over to town to a provision store to have the gold weighed. It lacked a fraction of being four dollars.

A short time after this, we moved down the McCosney.[32] I got sick and had a severe spell of diarrhea. I was not able to work for over a month. Sam and Mike were trying to prospect and locate a place to work.

One morning, they concluded to go down the river several miles, and they came to where there were some forty miners a mining. Heckard told those men that he and Sam would like to have some information in regard to mining and the country. These men advised them to go to the ravines and prospect. Although they then were dry, they said to get in the bed of the ravines and strip up the top dirt until you come to a change of color in the dirt or come to clay and gravel. Put as much of this in a sack or something and carry to water where you can pan it out; if you can find dirt, that will pan out ten cents to a pan of dirt—enough to pay to work. Then throw the waist dirt on one side of the gulch, smooth the bank off on the other side, and throw your pay dirt on this smooth strip in a little ridge. When the rainy season sets in, you can wash it out.

The men also said, "Build you a cabin where you are going to mine, and, if possible, get your winter's provision in before the rainy season sets in; for when the rains come, provision may get scarce and very high in the mines."

Sam seen an old Mexican that told him how to doctor me for my diarrhea. We had all the medicine or ingredients with us, which was brandy, opium, and gum of camphor, but I have forgotten how to proportion it. I was not to use any grease or salt in anything that I eat. All I ate for several days was quail roasted before the fire.

After Mike and Sam told the boys about the old miners and what they said, the next day they all went prospecting for a place for winter diggings. Finally, they selected a place about seven miles from where we were and about four miles from a little mining town called Fiddletown. Here the boys built a cabin to winter in. Henley Maddox and I stayed at the tent as we were not able to work, but we were able to wait on ourselves and cook a little.

---

32 According to Bayard Taylor's 1850 book *El Dorado*, page 172, the Cosumne River was pronounced by most as "Mokosumne," with an emphisized ee. (Elaine Zorbas, research librarian and Fiddletown historian in editor's correspondence, June 23, 2010)

FIDDLETOWN

As we had all concluded to try and follow the old miners' advice, Packard thought it best for us to buy a light wagon and a yoke of oxen to move around with, and to go to the city to buy and haul our provision. We bought the wagon and oxen the day before the boys went to build the cabin, taking the wagon and oxen with them. They were in a hurry to build the cabin so they would have a place for our provision. At the next place, they wanted to get the provision before the roads got muddy.

Soon as they got the roof on, someone came after Henley and I with the wagon and took our tools, tent, and the rest we had. We scraped all the money we had too, for Mike and Sam were going to start next morning to the city for provision. It took all the money that Bill and I had. We did not have enough to take a letter out of the office; the only time I was strapped was while I was there.

Mike and Sam got the provision alright. The boys finished up the cabin while Mike and Sam were gone. By this time, Henley and I had got stout enough to work a little. We then went to work, throwing out our pay dirt, which was quite a lot, and worked until the middle of November—still no rain. We got discouraged, for it was generally said that the rains set in from the first of October to the middle of November. We did not do anything for a few days but rove around.

One day, we all went to this Fiddletown,[33] and there were some men getting up a prospecting company to go eight miles southeast of town end prospect on a creek called Dry Creek. It was said that there was enough water to wash the dirt. Sam and Mike went with them, and in the course of three days, they all returned, bringing favorable news.

They found no miners or work done on this creek. They raised the company to forty. We went over, made a record, and established claims and by-laws, for we were the first mines on the creek. We built our cabins in a circle and kept guards out at nights for a while, as there was a big Indian town some eight miles from us. When we first went there, there was a report that the Indians were coming to drive us off. But they never came or molested us.

After building our cabins we staked off our claims and went to work. We built on a small valley. At the upper end of the valley there was a small canyon. After we had been there some two weeks, Bill Anderson and two more men proposed to go through and above this canyon on the creek prospecting. While there, they noticed a tent to the south of the creek near a ravine or gulch. They went to it and found some human bones. They immediately came in and reported.

We all went and found the hair of the head of two men as we supposed. One was sandy and the other dark. We found some of the bones but could not find all. The tent had holes in it, like arrow holes. We could not find a vestige of arms, tools, cooking utensils, or clothing, save the coat that was hanging in the tent. We gathered up all we could find, made a box, put them in, and buried them.

From the indications of everything, it went to prove that they had been there some time. They had almost worked out the gulch. The coat and tent was tender; and the claim did not look as it had been worked for some time; and no flesh about the bones. Some conjectured one thing and some another. I was there four months and when we come away, there was no key to unlock the mystery.

———————————✦———————————

33 According to Elaine Zorbas, head of Research at the Pasadena Public Library and historian of Fiddletown, by conversation with the editor: Robert Clark's mention of being in Fiddletown in that year may be the earliest documentation of the name "Fiddletown" being used for that mining area. Historians previously knew it was settled by Missourians [Zorbas, p. 19], but R. Clark's account provides earlier documented evidence of the name.

HUNTING

We six boys were all the Missourians there—of the forty that first went over.[34] They were all Eastern men and knew nothing at all about hunting. As there was no butcher shop there and considerable blacktail deer on the hills and mountains, we six boys got to hunting quite a bit. In fact, we hunted a good deal the first two months we were there. We could sell all our meat to the other boys for twenty-five cents per pound. Our claims yielded us tolerable fair wages, and we wanted to get the work worked out by the first of March so we could go north to the rivers for the summer. We changed the hunting program: instead of all hunting, two went each morning, and we took it in rotation.

We had got acquainted with a young man by the name of Tom Armstrong, and he would frequently come to our cabin after supper and spend the evening. It so happened that he came one evening, and next morning was brother Sam's and my time to go a hunting. We happened to speak of it in the presence of Tom. He remarked that he would like very much to go [because he] would like to kill a deer or see one killed, but knew nothing about hunting. I proposed to take my gun and go with Sam. He said he would. Sam told him to come early, that he wanted to start at day.

Next morning, Tom was on hand. They started at day[break]. As Sam stepped out, he called to me and said, "I am going north this morning; and if we kill a deer, we will take it to Fiddletown and sell it, so

---

34 The forty being the miners who formed the company to work Dry Creek.

you need not be uneasy if we do not get back today." [Later,] they told me that after they went up in the peaks, they saw four deer near a peak. Sam told Tom to go around and get on the opposite side of the peak. Sam would try to slip up close enough to get a shot and would wait until Tom got around, for him to keep a sharp lookout; for the deer would be very apt, whether he got a shot or not. So Sam crawled until he thought he had a good chance. When he shot, his deer turned from the shaprill[35] down a steep incline; the others took around the peak. Sam said he heard Tom shoot. Sam went to look after his deer. Tom said he went after his, for he was sure he hit it.

The boys got separated, and it began to snow. They had a regular snow storm up in the mountains. The snow got so thick that they could not see. They lost their course and could not find each other. Sam said he shot his gun several times but could not hear Tom. Finally, he struck a trail and thought he was right, but he saw some Indians that acted so strange that he got in a canyon and walked all night back and forth to keep from freezing. Tom kept on up the side of the mountain and got so excited that he walked and ran until he gave out and sometime in the night sat down on a log.

As good luck for Tom, the next morning some hunters went up the mountain to look for game and found Tom, though unconscious. They took him to camp and gave him all the help they could, and by ten or eleven o'clock, he was able to tell them where he belonged and his name. Then they sent a runner to tell us.

As the boys did not get in that evening, we thought they had gone to Fiddletown and was not uneasy. At noon, Bill and I went to dinner, and the boys had not come yet. I felt uneasy but went back to work. In a short time, I said to Bill that there was something wrong with the boys, or they would be here. I could not work and had to see something about them. I decided I was going to Fiddletown to see if they had been there. As we were going to the cabin, I kept watching the road that came from Fiddletown, and away up on the side of the mountain, I saw Sam coming.

---

35 Chapparal: an area of dry land with low-growing shrubs and trees.

We waited until he came down, and as he came near, I saw something was wrong, for he had such a strange, worn haggard look. I said, "Sam, what's the matter?"

He said nothing. I then asked him where Tom was. He said, "Isn't Tom in?"

I told him that we had not heard of them since they left. He then told how they had parted and for me to tell all the rest [of the men].

He was so tired, so I took him to the cabin. When we got there, the runner had come with news from Tom. This seemed to help Sam. We were all so sorry to hear of Tom's fate. His partners made preparations and started after him the next morning.

They got in with him that evening, but he could not walk. His feet and hands were badly frozen. The last time that I saw Tom, he could not use his hands much. They were so stiff and drawn. He was fifteen miles from home when found.

Sam had nothing to eat since the morning they left. He said that he stayed in his canyon until after sunrise. It being clear, he climbed to a peak, took his bearings, got his course, and started for home. He took a severe cold and was not able to work for some time. This was the last hunt we had.

Now we all went to work to clean up our claims. That is, Bill, Sam and I worked together, and Heckard, Gatewood and Maddox were partners. In working, we struck a lead that run under our cabin. We followed it through, dug, threw the dirt and rock back, and leveled up and sold the shack for fifty dollars. We got our claims worked before Heckard got theirs.

Sam and I concluded to go and wash some of the dirt that we threw out in the fall. The dirt turned out well, but we had to carry the water so far that we gave up. That season was dry: [only a] little rain in the valleys, but snow in the mountains until the snow melted.

Heckard soon cleaned out their claim, and we were about ready to pull for the city—we all had to go there to start.

MISSOURI TEAM SEPARATES

I forgot to say that we sold our wagon and oxen when we first moved here. This proved to be a pleasant place to winter, for the ice was not heavy enough on the creek to bear up a goose at any time.

We sold all our tools and guns and walked to the city, called "seventy-five miles." The second afternoon after getting to the city, we parted with Heckard, Bill Anderson, Gatewood and Maddox as they wanted to go up the Feather River[36] and Sam and I up the south fork of the American River.

We parted the best of friends, but I never saw Mike, Carson, or Henley Maddox anymore. Bill came home, and I saw him. Mike came also, but I never met him. Gatewood and Maddox never came and have all gone to that Great Beyond.[37]

After parting with the boys, Sam and I felt lonely but concluded not to start until the next morning. So, we began to look for someone that we knew, and soon met with Bob Gosney, a Marion County boy and now

---

36 Johannes Sutter (Swiss immigrant who fled his country to escape debtor's prison) obtained 50,000+ acres (which he called New Helvetia) near the meeting of the Sacramento and American Rivers from the Mexican governor prior to California becoming part of the United States. This meeting of the rivers became the city of Sacramento in 1849, and the Sacramento River's name was changed to the Feather River.

37 An account of the gold rush in the *History of Marion County* reference notes that a James Maddox, son of William Maddox of Ralls County, returned June 16, 1851 with cholera upon arriving in Hannibal and died the next day. This is not Henley Maddox (son of Basil Maddox) but still interesting to note the impact the travels took upon populations and the magnitude of cholera.

a brother-in-law of mine.[38] We soon fell into conversation. He told us that he had just closed a deal with a man from Jackson County, Missouri, by the name of James Price. This man Price had gone out in forty-nine and made some money by hauling and selling provisions in the mines; but by some misdeal, he had lost all but two wagons and six yoke of oxen. Price proposed to Bob that he would give him a lien on the teams and wagons if he would load the wagons with provisions and take them up the American River to a place called Barnes Barr to start a provision store.

Bob said he had just finished leading the wagons and paid for the goods. Sam remarked that is where we wanted to go. Bob said, "Come down here, where Price is." We went, and Bob introduced us and told Price where we were from and how we were thinking of going to Barnes Barr. Price said, "There is good diggings up there and some rich river claims." That pleased Sam, for he wanted to get in a river claim somehow. Then Price said, "Boys, come and go with us, and if you want to take any provisions, put it on the wagon, and we will help each other."

We consented and bought a sack of flour and some meat and other things. We left the city that evening as Price wanted to take his cattle where they could get grass. Jim Price had a half-brother by the name of Alf Henson that drove one team for Jim. We all went in company and had a very nice trip, but on a very rough road. We made it all right.

There was a big house on top of the mountain where we had to go down to the bar on the river. We left the wagons and goods there with Alf, and we all walked down and stayed there that night. They said there had never been a wagon down that mountain. That night Jim made arrangements with a free darkey that ran a bakery and eating house in order to put his goods there until he could put up a canvas house for the goods.

Next morning, we all went to bring the goods down. The way Jim arranged it was, he had us cut some small pine trees, cut out the tops, then take three or four tops, lash them together with ropes and chains, and cut and mat in the limbs. After that, he had us pack and tie the goods

---

38 Robert Clark married Sarah Jane Gosney, daughter of Robert and Martha (Morgan) Gosney, 27 October 1853. She died 28 January 1905 and is buried in Mt. Vernon Cemetery, Marion County. She joined the Methodist Church South in fall of 1848; Robert joined in 1858 in Mercer.

with ropes. In this way, he made two drags and hitched three yoke of oxen to each to drag them down. Bob Gosney did not like the prospect and proposed to sell out to Sam. At last, they accomplished a trade that day. We soon had a canvas house up and the goods moved in. Sam did not like the business, and as soon as he could make his money back, he sold out.

He was engaged in this six or eight weeks. He made several trips to the city and sold pretty well out, and he let Jim have the rest pretty cheap. A few days after Sam closed up with Price, a Mr. Oliver came to Price to get him to do some hauling.

This man, Oliver, was from Jackson County, and I think he was an acquaintance of the Prices at home. The hauling that he wished done was timber for a dam and flume. Price turned to Sam and said, "If you and Bob will haul it, you can have the wagons and teams, for I will not be using them." Oliver said he would give one hundred dollars for the job. We told him we would do the work as the teams were not costing us anything.

THE OLIVER TEAM

On Monday, we went with the teams. The timber was on the mountain on the opposite side of the river. He had the timber all chopped and hands to help load and unload. We did not have to move the timber very far; we walked as far down as was safe, turned, and unloaded with the logs lying across the hill. We hauled the logs in four days, but we were one day going and one day coming, consuming one week.

The evening we finished, Mr. Oliver said, "Now boys, I will pay you the hundred dollars, or I will let you have a seventh interest in the claim." We told him we would think the matter over and concluded if he would take one as shareholder and give the other work by the day that we would make the trade. When we made our proposition known to Mr. Oliver, he said he would do it. Sam was booked as shareholder and I as hired hand, at five dollars per day.

Mr. Oliver, I learned, had a brother that had taken cattle across the plains in 'Fifty, along with two sons, lads large enough to help drive the cattle. Soon after getting to California, Oliver['s brother] took sick and died. When the widow here in Jackson County[39] received the intelligence, Wain Oliver agreed to go and see after her sons to determine what disposal

---

39 This reference probably is for Jackson County, Missouri, for which Kansas City serves as the county seat. This, then, is not to be confused with Jackson, a city in Amador County, California, which began in 1848 as a center for gold mining and cattle. [https://www.ci.jackson.ca.us/] Family records note that some of Clark's offspring moved to other states, and at the time of writing his memoir, presumably 1903 or a few years before, Clark may have been residing with one offspring in Kansas City.

was made of the cattle. Wain came out by water and found the boys not far from this place, but the cattle were in jeopardy some way. I rather think there was a claim of partnership; at all events, Oliver never realized anything for the cattle.

Wain Oliver was a man of considerable means. After looking around and figuring some, he concluded to stay and try mining one summer. He bought this claim out, and out himself. The claim had only been prospected but reckoned a fine prospect. Wain wanted to give the two boys a chance to make something, [so] he gave them one share apiece; and sold four shares with ours at one hundred dollars a share, making seven shares in all.

Oliver had some money, and he promised us, need be, he would put it all in the claim and wait until taken out of the claim. There was a claim just above ours called Kibby claim, and there were several Jackson County men in it. Our claim was called the Oliver claim. We all agreed to work under one dam and, under the circumstances, could not do otherwise.

Both parties were to do an equal portion of the work. First, we went and got the timber down the mountain for the dam, and on the eighth day of May, we commenced work in the water: putting in the dam, some putting in timber, and some boating dirt and rock. They made a small flat boat to boat dirt and rock. The water was so cold coming from the snow on the mountains [it] would make our lips blue.

The Kibby boys had the advantage of us in situation of the claims, for theirs gave them room to carry their water in a race;[40] but rock came in to bluff on ours, so there was no room for a race. Consequently, we took the water from the end of their race in a flume. The Kibby boys went to work on their claim long before we got our flume done. Their claim had lots of fell, so they could work as soon as they turned the race. In fact, they drained most all by throwing in a sack dam at the foot of their claim. This is done by making canvas sacks and filling them with sand; it holds the water back.

I will now try and tell how we got our timber from where Sam and I hauled it. As I have tried to refrain from telling big stories, I reckon I am due one. The timber was near a half-mile from the river at the head

––––––––––––––––

40 Race: a fast stream of water in a channel.

of the gulch. The sides of the gulch and bottom were mostly rock. We cleared the loose rock out, turned the log, big end first, and gave it a start. Away it would plunge down, throwing rock here and there, and sometimes one would run clear through and not stop until it plunged into the river. When one lodged, it would be apt to lodge on another. Sometimes we would have three or four lodged. We would have to keep a sharp lookout when we went to loosen them. Some of these logs were sixty feet long. The hardest comes now.

One day, we turned one of these long logs loose, and she made a terrible clatter on the rocks but stopped all of a sudden. We went to see, and from the looks, we supposed it struck solid rock on one side of the gulch and bounded and struck a live oak tree, end foremost, fifteen feet up from the ground, splitting the log far enough so it hung by the split on the tree. I will try and help you out on this some. The place was very steep here and the tree was several feet in front of where the log struck and bounded. To take it on a level it would not be so high as to take it from the root of the tree, but the log split all the same. We moved all the logs down in three days.

Now things looked blue for the boys of the Oliver claim, and each shareholder was sixty dollars apiece in debt for provisions alone besides using up all of Mr. Oliver's money. This may seem a little strange. I will try and explain. You remember how I said Mr. Oliver promised us, if need be, he would put in his last dollar and wait until taken out of the claim, and he did. We boys would have never seen the bottom of that claim if it had not been for Wain Oliver. The way the provision bill came was this: Oliver bought a week's provisions at a time and did all of our trading with a man by the name of Knight. One Saturday evening, Oliver went for the next week's supply and took me to help carry it home. After we bought the provisions, he remarked to Mr. Knight that he would pay for it, but he did not know where the next was to come from. Then, Knight asked Oliver how they were getting along with the claim, and the two had quite a conversation. I heard Knight say, "Well, I will be up there Monday morning." Mr. Knight came up as he promised.

We were at work on the flume, and they looked over the work then came where we were. Mr. Oliver said, "Boys, Mr. Knight wishes to speak to all of you." Mr. Knight then said, "Mr. Oliver tells me your money is running short, and I propose to furnish your provisions and wait until you take it out of this claim. You have to promise to pay me the first money you take out." And of course we made the promise. That is how the shareholders came to be in debt.

As the pumps did not accomplish what we wanted, all hands were at a loss to know just what to do. There was a small bar formed just below where this bedrock cropped out, and the river made a bar extending to the end of the flume. Finally, a man by the name of Woodard, another shareholder, proposed to work the bar. All hands agreed to the proposition. As there was not very much fall in the river, here the water that came from the flume flowed back on some of the bar. Oliver thought it best to throw in a rock dam to keep the water back. We got the canvas, and all hands went to making and filling sacks. Soon enough, we had a dam. We did not have to make a very high one to keep the water back. We got ready to get to work on Monday, the second week in September. That morning we stripped a place—that is, shoveled off the sand and loose rocks—and set our flume and went to working. At night, [we] cleaned up and weighed our gold, and we had three hundred dollars. Next morning, we started Sam Beckum to the city to hire hands. He was gone three days. When he returned, we had twelve hundred dollars. Beckum hired each shareholder a hand, making fifteen in all. There were seven shareholders, [each with seven hands] making fourteen. I was a Company hand, making [the total] fifteen people. But young Oliver cooked, leaving fourteen to mine [for gold]. The next morning, after Sam Beckum and hands got in, we set another flume and ran two flumes. A thirty-foot flume gives five hands good room to work on each side: two to shovel and one to stand at the riddle to wash and shovel rock off the riddle.

There were ten at the flumes and four to shovel off, two for each flume. For three days in succession, the fourteen hands took out seven hundred dollars a day; we never took less than three hundred. There was a deep hole of water that we were very anxious to drain. It was near forty yards long and averaged from eight to twelve feet deep before we turned the water in, and here is where we wanted to work; but next morning, there was no water running in the bed of the creek. But in this hole, water stood from four to six feet deep, and the bedrock creeped out at the lower end level with the water, so there was no way to ditch and drain it.

After viewing the situation, Oliver proposed to try pumps on it. So, they engaged a carpenter, a sort of genius, to make pumps. He made and put in twelve pumps and two water wheels. He put the wheels in the flume, attached two lone cranks to the wheels, set six pumps together, three on a side, and attached the crank to the pump in such a way so as the crank came up with the other pumps and wheels. The power was given from the water running in the flume. Each pump would throw a bucket of water at each stroke. They run night and day, but it would not do. We could not bring the water low enough so as we could work. It seemed that the water fed into this hole from crevices from the race above. We got live oak for posts to set the flume on. It is a timber that will sink in water. The way we arranged it, we first cut mortises in the streamers, a certain number of feet apart. Then we cut a tenant on the post, fastened one of the streamers next to the flume, floated it where we wanted it, and sank the post end down, opposite mortise. That way it don't take much to raise it in the water high enough to slip the tenant in place. [Then, we'd] halve the streamers at the end half and half one on the other, put the ties on and set props.

The flume was twelve feet wide, three feet high at sides, and all pine except the posts. It took thirteen thousand feet of lumber to bend it. The lumber was all green pine, two-inch straight edge lumber. In laying it down, we keyed it up as close as we could. When done laying the floor, they bought canvas by the bolt, cut it in four-inch strips and tethered those strips over the joints of the plank in the floor and sides of the flume. We finished it, after so long a time, and opened the floodgate to let the water in, slowly watching and bracing where we thought a weak place was. Finally, they let the water all in, which filled the flume almost full.

That night we did not sleep much, but sat up and watched to see that the flume did not cram, but the next morning, we felt proud to see her standing straight and solid. But our time was short, for there came a rise in the river on the third of October, and by night, the water was slopping over the flume so that we had to shut it off into the bed of the river.

I do not think there was ever a set of boys that ever put in a harder summer's work than we did on that claim—lifting those heavy timbers and handling that green pine lumber; but we kept well and stout. Sometimes, one would get hurt and lay off a day or so, but California is as good a climate as can be found. We boys would work all day in the water and, at night, wrap up in our blankets with our wet clothes on, lie down under a live oak tree, and sleep all night. Next morning, we would get up as bright and sound as a dollar, as the saying is, with no sore joints, headaches or any dull feelings—and no electric storms or cyclones that I heard of.

I said we all kept well. I had a touch of something like scurvy right in the wind up, caused by living on salt vitals[41] so long. It was on Saturday evening that we shut the water off the flume, and by Sunday morning, there were four that had sold their share in the claim. The three Olivers— Wain, Bill, and Stokes— and Boutwell were in our claim, and in the Kibby claim, there was Jim Brown, Jim Halcom, Steve Thurston, Pete Kiethley.[42]

---

41 colloquialism, "vittles"— the word *victuals*, meaning food

42 In the Clark memoir, the spelling is Kiethley; The Kiethley Cemetery is located in Ralls county, south of Hannibal and east of New London

TO SAN FRANCISCO

We were all sure that the rainy season was setting in. The boys were all fixing to start for the city that afternoon. A few days before the rise, Sam and I had been talking about my coming home soon; for, said he, "I fear if you stay much longer you will get down sick." I said I did not want to come and leave him, and I asked him if I stayed until the next March if he would then come. He said he would.

I thought no more of coming, but [my condition] was gradually getting worse. The boys were fixing their gold in belts. Sam said, "Bob you had as well fix and go with the boys."

"Yes," said Wain and Stokes, "We will take care of you."

I then said, "Sam promised the other day to go with me if I would stay until March."

Sam said, "Yes, you stay until you get down under the doctor's care, and maybe take all we both have."

So, I consented and got ready. I left the mines Oct. 4, 1851. I was in California for a little over thirteen months, and mined all the time I was there.

I was in Sacramento twice, spent about three days each time. Gambling was carried on with a high hand in the cities. And, in the mines, all kinds of games and tricks were bet on. There were two large gambling houses in Sacramento City called the Eldorado and Diannah. One had twenty-five and the other four gambling tables. The houses were gotten up especially for that purpose: a costly bar, a fine-finished stage where the band played and sang music. Male and female singers of talent were there. The walls were decorated with flashy pictures, and the bar was arranged in art with bottles of sparkling wines and liquors. And the glittering gold piled on the gambling tables, saying by these influences, "Here is ease, here is wealth," inviting the young man in and away from the path of truth, honesty, and virtue. And from the sacred influences of that fond mother, who taught the infant's lips to say, "Now I lay me down to sleep, I pray the Lord my soul to keep." But oh, to hear the oaths, the clank of glass and money at the bar, and the chink of money at the tables was enough to chill the blood.

Oh, young man, I wish it proclaimed from pole to pole: "Never, no never, gamble. It invites most all other vices: drinking, swearing, cheating, lying, stealing and murder. What profit a man if he gain the whole world and lose his own soul?"[43]

When we got to Sacramento, the news was current that cholera was very bad at different places on the way home. Mr. Knight was with us on his way home in New Orleans, and he said that he was acquainted with an officer in San Francisco, on the line to New Orleans. He said if we bought a ticket for him, he would go and ascertain the facts. So, he went that evening and came back next morning, reporting favorably. That evening, we all went down to San Francisco.

There were two packets that ran in opposition between San Francisco and Sacramento at that time. That evening, both had a full cabin of passengers. Both pulled out near the same time, and we had a boat race. The passengers got interested, and all got on deck with much cheering, waving handkerchiefs and clapping hands—sometimes side by side. But it so happened that our boat led the way.

When Wain Oliver went out, he traveled on a sail vessel all the way and had a fine trip, and he saved money compared to what a through ticket on the steamers cost. Through tickets then cost three hundred dollars from San Francisco to New York or New Orleans. Wain Oliver insisted we would save money to come on a sail vessel. We looked around and found a vessel that had just been fit up for passengers. The officers said she would

---

43 From Mark 8:36 and Matthew 16:26, New Testament Bible.

sail in a day or so to San Wan Del Nort on the Nicaragua route.[44]   This route was not established then, or there was not any steamers on that line.

The next day, Wain Oliver, Stokes Oliver, Pete Kiethley, Steve Thurston and I went to the docks where the vessel lay. We went aboard, looked through her cabin, and bought tickets to San Wan Del Nort; but I have forgotten what they cost. As soon as we bought tickets and got the number of our berth, that was our home. We ate and slept on board, but the ship did not sail for eight or ten days after we bought our tickets. When I got to the city, I got some medicine, and a change of diet soon brought me all right.

The ship was a three-mast vessel, and she was called *The Lowell*. I do not know how many men there were in officers and crew. There were sixty-five passengers on board and considerable cargo. She was expecting to go to some of the islands after she left San Wan.

The reason I cannot give dates, along here, I was trusting to my diary, which I intended to keep on my way home, but I lost it at Havana, Cuba; consequently, [I] did not charge my mind and I will have to write entirely from memory.

---

44 San Juan del Norte, also known as Greytown, is now San Juan de Nicaragua. It is located at the mouth of the San Juan River that begins at San Carlos on the southeast end of Lake Nicaragua (Lago Cocibolca) and empties into the Caribbean Sea, near the border with Costa Rica.

PACIFIC OCEAN VOYAGE

I think about the ninth morning after we went aboard, the captain gave order to set the sails and weigh anchor, and then we knew we would soon try the ocean. She had her clean, white sails set, and the breeze was just strong enough to fill all her sails. She circled around in the bay and came up alongside of the wharf where our friends were standing. [She] gave a salute then sheared off for the Golden Gate. The passengers were all on deck, waving handkerchiefs and shouting goodbye to friends and California. The sailors were busy setting sails and tightening ropes, and the first mate, a crusty old fellow, was giving orders. The passengers would be in the way of the sailors. Finally, I heard the mate say, "Thank God, I bet some of this will stop when we get out through the gate." I did not know what he meant but suspected something ahead and kept a lookout. Sure enough, pretty soon I felt the old ship give a different motion. It felt like it was lifting you up, and then you would sink away down like a high, long swing. The old ocean waves had pretty large, heavy swells that morning. Pretty soon a fellow would crawl to the gunnell, stick his head over, and heave Jonah awhile, then crawling off saying, "Oh, how sick I am." The mate would look at him with a grin and say, "I thought so."

I was never seasick nor missed a meal the trip through. After we were out several days, our water got very bad. They say that fresh water at sea will die then purify. I know ours smelled as though it might be dead, but after a week, it got good. One morning, our water was so bad; a small cloud came up, and we watched it, hoping it would rain for drinking water. As we kept looking, there was a streak formed at the edge of the cloud down to the water that looked something like those streaks that we call *the sun drawing water.* Soon after it struck, the white caps began to fly, and spray began to go around and up—it seemed into the edge of the cloud. The captain said it was two miles away, but he sheared the vessel away from it.

It rained a shower, and we got some rainwater to drink. We had an old sea captain aboard besides the captain of the ship. He claimed that he was working for a New York ship company and that the company was engaged in sending ships around Cape Horn to San Francisco, selling out to those fellows that were running the Chile trade. He had been around with one and was on his way back to take charge of another one in the spring. His name was Downing, a jolly soul. His bunk was just above mine, so we soon got acquainted, and he has told me many a sea story.

The afternoon of the shower was threatening and looked stormy. A strong wind blew from the southwest. It being a favorable point of compass to advance us more swiftly, the captain had a full sail up. By six o'clock it was thundering in the West and looked as though a storm was approaching. The ship was making such fine speed that it was with reluctance that the captain would call down a sail. Finally, there came a lull for a minute. Captain Downing was lying on his bunk, and I had just laid down when the heavy wind struck. It came a little northwest and caught the ship with most of her sails unfurled, cramming her to one side so much that the chairs in the cabin slid over. The captain of the vessel and crew were all on deck when the ship did not balance up. Captain Downing sprung out of his bunk. When he struck the floor, I jumped too and caught his belt. He opened the cabin door but it took both to shut it, and he locked the door. When we got out, the water was running on the deck; but it was so dark we could see but little, only by the lightning. Between the cabin door and main mast was the hatchway that led down where the steerage passengers were. When we got near the hatch, we saw the door was open and water running down the hatchway. Downing threw the door shut and locked it, and then we came to the mast. The first word that passed between us was, "Here, young man; hold to that rigging." I let go of the belt, caught the ropes and swung on.

Downing then ran to the pilot house. Then, by the lightning, I saw him come back towards the forecastle. Captain Downing told me about it after it was all over. Downing said, when he got to the pilot house, there was no one there at the wheel. Then he ran forward and called to the captain and asked what was the matter. The first mate was on the first main arm, and the second mate and the crew were in the rigging but doing nothing. In answer to his question, the captain said, "Captain Downing, I give you the command to take the trumpet. They can't hear me, and to use the trumpet, I can't speak plain enough." The captain of the ship was badly hair-lipped, hence the confusion.

Downing took the trumpet, and I heard his first command: "Let all halyards fly!" I cannot tell you what sails it was but I know there was a terrible popping and cracking amongst the sails. He then took two men and rigged a block and tackle to the wheel. It took them all to turn the rudder. I reckon it was then that I felt her straighten up. When she began to ride the waves, I had to hold to my ropes. Now, there came a cry from below from those steerage passengers. When she would strike a heavy wave, she would tremble. This caused the passengers to think there was trouble; and finding that they were locked up, seeing the water on the floor that run down the hatchway, and hearing the fresh water joshling in the casks beneath them in the hole, they thought a leak had busted, [was] filling the hole, and rising up on them.

Some of them became almost panic-stricken and crowded up to the hatch door, calling for the captain and the mate, begging most piteously to be let out. By the time the thunder had somewhat abated, sails were whipped to pieces or torn away, and others furled and yards squared around. things had become more quiet. Downing and the mate passed where I was pulling on the ropes. I heard Downing say, "Now mate, take your lantern and see how things are below." That was where I felt interested, for I felt that if she was filling with water below, hope was gone. When they came to the hatch, the captain unlocked the door and said, "Are you ready?" As he threw the door back, the mate, with one hand on the side, threw himself down as far as he could and called out, "Oh yes, this is what I have been wanting to see…you have been drinking your good whiskey and cursing. Pray now, pray d___it, pray soon." As soon as he saw he had their attention, he motioned his hand and said, "Please stand aside and let me down." They all obeyed. As he moved down, Downing closed the door and not one got out. The mate went down to the bottom of the vessel and examined it, and came back; and [he] explained how it all occurred, and how the water came to be on the floor, and quieted the passengers.

The mate came, and I heard him say, "She is leaking some but not dangerous. I guess we had better start the pumps." There was not much sleep that night.

At day we all lay down to try and rest some but the sea was rough, and quite a gale blowing. Yet, the ship kept running with the gale, for the sea was too rough and the wind too high to tack back and forth.

About sunrise, we heard the cry from the watchmen, "A wreck!" All hands jumped from their bunks and ran on deck. Off to our left, we could once in a while see the hull of a vessel as the waves would toss it up. Our ship ran as near as she dare on account of the rough sea and strong gale, but we could not see a soul on the wreck. She was a two-masted vessel, and as the waves would toss her up, we could read her name, which was the *Oak Leaf*. We supposed by the appearance that when the storm struck her, she had a full set of sails up, and the storm was so heavy that it twisted the masts off near the masthead, dropping across the hull and hanging on the stumps by splinters. The vessel filled with water. The waves were running so high, and the wind so strong, that the captains said it was impossible to board her.

This storm struck us right off from Cape St. Lucus and drove us away to sea. The seawater possessed something that makes it sparkle and look like fire when thrown in spray after night; so that night of the storm, it looked to me like a vast prairie on fire.

I think there was about ten days after the storm until we saw land. On our trip, I saw different kinds of fish and sea animals, from a flying fish up to a whale. One morning, off to our right, we saw a whale spouting water. He was too far to be seen good. We could partially see his head and the water spouting. Captain Downing was on deck a good deal after night, and if anything unusual occurred, he would be sure to come after me to see it. One night, he came into the cabin in a great hurry and awoke me and said, "Jump up and come out, for there is a great shoal of porpoise out here." I went, and it did look pretty. The water was smooth, and I had a good chance to see them. They would jump out of the water two or three feet high, kind of snort or blow (you have heard the expression, blow like a porpoise), and skim the water deep enough to break the surface. It would show, like long streaks of fire, in all directions and as far as you could see.

We caught some fish that were good to eat. The dolphin is a beautiful fish. One evening, we caught one of those fish nearly three feet long. It made a mess for all of the cabin passengers.

I have heard that old sailors once believed that if a shark followed a vessel, it was taken that someone on board would soon die. I believe that if they follow a vessel, it is a token that they want the waste that is thrown from the table. We were in several shoals of flying fish. They are generally from eight to twelve inches long.

Speaking of shark, I have a little shark story to tell. One day, there were three sharks that had been around the vessel all day, picking up the scraps that were thrown out. In the afternoon, five or six of us boys asked a sailor to harpoon one of them for us. He finally said that he would, but that we would have to take him out to get his harpoon and rope. We fixed the rope, tied one end to the guards of the vessel, set the barb of the harpoon, and waited. Soon, one came slowly up, and when he got in reach, the sailor made his throw and planted the harpoon square in his back. The barb struck deep and held him fast. "Now get my harpoon," said the sailor. The shark was plunging and splashing the water every way. One said, "Let him run until he tired down." Now, the shaft of this harpoon was three or four feet long of half-inch iron rod. The shark made a dart and ran the full length of the rope. It gave a flounce and rolled the shaft around him like a hoop. Then we got ahold of the rope and tried to pull him in, but he would flop around. We could not get him over on deck, for we were afraid to get close to him. Finally, the sailor got us some iron hooks that we could strike into him and hold, and the sailor helped get him on deck. Then we butchered and dissected him. He was six feet long. They have saw-like teeth. By the time we got through, the mate got after us. We cleaned up and were tired.

We were in several calms whilst on board. To get in a calm at sea in a hot climate, not have breeze enough to give the ship steerage, sails flopping and hanging straight down, the masts and the ship wallowing around the bow—first one way and then another—wasn't very pleasant traveling. We were in a calm three days, and the sun was very hot.

One day, we hove in sight of a little town; although, we ran under a headwind and had to tack[45] back and forth to get up at sunset. We were near enough to see the men walking around in town, and three men came to us in a little boat. One said he was a pilot and had come out to pilot us in, but the captain would not engage him. By this time, they began to light up in town. There was no lighthouse or anything of that sort. By this time, the steward announced supper.

All hands were in glee and went to supper, as we thought for the last time on the *The Lowell*. But when we came on deck from supper, it was dark, and they had lost sight of the lights on shore. The captain gave orders to run up close to the wind as they could and keep tacking back and forth. At this time, the pilot that came to us slipped out with his oarsman and left the other man with us.

Next morning, we were all up at day and out on deck, the ship still tacking back and forth; but when the captain made his reckoning, he found that we were about twenty miles to sea. About nine o'clock. a breeze sprung up from the sea, and we pulled for the shore. But the breeze soon dropped and left us in calm with heavy swells,[46] slowly drifting towards a reef of big rock; and all hands began to feel fearful when they could not reach anchorage yet.

At this time, some of the passengers got very uneasy. Then, the man that came on board proposed that he could take some six or eight in his boat to shore. Some of the passengers wanted to know what he would charge. He said he would take them for ten dollars apiece if they would help pull the oars. They soon made a party of six, I think, got in, and pulled for the shore. They had not been gone for long when a cloud shot up like a little shower; and pretty soon, a breeze came. We scud out from there.

As the cloud came nearer, the wind got stronger and we soon overtook the skiff. The boys were pulling the oars for dear life. Soon after passing them, there came a hard dash of wind and rain, and the

------

45 hove: in view of; tack: the process of changing the direction of a ship by adjusting the sails.

46 Today, the Pacific Ocean beach line near San Juan del Sur is known for its great surfing for sport enthusiasts.

captain said, "I fear them boys will have trouble. Shall I try to pick them up?" Some of the passengers said, "Go on captain; our lives are as dear as theirs are. Go in while you can." But it soon slacked, and we ran in and got anchorage.

NICARAGUA

We finished our trip across the isthmus and came to an old Spanish Town called San Carless[47] at about two o'clock. We had very good weather here.

We stayed there several days. Why? I cannot tell. Our landlord, we called a Dutch Jew; but I do not know of what nationality. The houses were large but not tall. They were built of sun-dried brick and covered with tile.

There was a large Catholic Church here. The belfry was arranged somewhat different from the American churches—not nearly so tall. I guess the reason they built them was on account of earthquakes and volcano shocks. The bells on the churches were made stationary, three on a church, one large and two small ones. Two men did nothing but tend and beat the bells. They had something made like drumsticks, but I supposed they were metal. The man that beat the small one had two, and they could beat a kind of tune on those bells. They beat them night and day, I believe, at intervals. And there were other men that stayed there all the time: the usher, the man that veiled and unveiled the images and

---

47 Today's city of San Carlos is midway across the isthmus at the southeast corner of Lake Nicaragua (Lago Cocibolca) near the San Juan River, which divides today's Nicaragua from Costa Rica. San Juan del Sur is 12 miles below Rivas; it is a fishing village. The town of "Rivas" is on the west edge of Lake Nicaragua Northwest of the Lake, above Lake Managua and near the Pacific coast, is "volcano row." Mark Twain's account of his travels from San Francisco through Nicaragua notes they landed at San Juan del Sur, which is along the Pacific coast. San Juan del Sur Bay and the surrounding shoreline is formed by hilly rock cliffs. (Twain, *Autobiography*, 2013)

waited on the altar, and others. I do not know how many.

The second day we were there, we noticed the natives coming to church in most all streets. Someone asked if they would let Americans come in church. "Yes," said the landlord, "if you behave and don't laugh and make fun." Then about six of us concluded to go. There was a young Dutchman traveling with us that noticed us when we got near the church, and he asked where we were going. We told him we were going to church. He said he would go too. He wished to come up to us before we entered the church, and he ran.

When we came to the door the usher met us. We raised our hats and walked in, the usher going before. When we had gotten several paces from the door, here came our Dutchman bolting in, hat on. But he hadn't made many steps in when two of those big natives grabbed him, back down several steps and let him down. And the other natives came running and got around him, stomping their feet, pointing up with their fingers, their hands waving around and around, their heads thrown back as if looking upward crying, "Crah-ho, crah-ho."[48] Then they dropped on their knees and threw the dirt and dust up over their heads. The usher asked us if that man was with us. One of our men said he is traveling with us but meant no harm in what he done. Then the usher said we had better go out there.

We went out, the usher with us. He called to the natives to stop and told them in their language what we said and finally got them quieted. The usher said the Dutchman could go back to the hotel but must not go back to the church. The Dutchman did not want to go to church then but gladly went back to the hotel.

The fourth morning after coming to San Carless, we paid our bill and moved down to Old Revous, which is about eight miles east of San Carless. This is a very old town. Some of the boys said they were told that

---

48 Worshippers were probably saying "carajo..." which was slang that harshly directed the unwelcomed guest to "get out of here!" Or, perhaps a plea for cleansing of the church. Apparently, the wearing of the hat was insulting. The expletive stems from sailing terminology. The carajo is the lookout basket on top of the mast of a sailship, a position where one could develop seasickness easily. Captains sent sailors to the carajo as punishment. Today, to say "go to carajo" is considered a severe curse on someone and is rather vulgar.

there had not been a house built for three hundred years. It had quite an ancient appearance. I could not judge why they built their houses so large. One day, I was walking around looking at the old ruins, for there was a number of those old houses evidently thrown down by earthquakes or volcano shocks. I came on to one that had a foundation with one hundred steps.[49]   It was evident that this old house had been in ruins a long time. There, around the ruins of that old mansion, was the largest orange trees that I had ever seen. They showed to be very old yet vigorous: no dead limbs on them, a fine crop of ripe oranges on the branches. Around this town, the orange trees grew out on the commons, and I have thought they were the biggest and sweetest I ever ate.

I have wondered what use they made of those large buildings. I can't imagine what the Spaniards wanted them for, and the natives were too lazy to utilize them for anything.[50]   What few inhabitants I saw on the isthmus, I thought they were Spaniards and Mexicans. But those poor ignorant, lazy creatures around San Carless and Revous, I do not know what blood they are.[51] They are of a yellow, swarthy, dirty looking pieces of humanity, and I think they live principally on fruit and what grows spontaneously in that tropical country. I saw two or three patches of corn on the slope as we came down from the isthmus, but I think it belonged to Mexicans. Those fellows around Lake Nicaragua are of a darker color and active. They are great water dogs. Their little children swim like ducks, as the saying is.

---

49 Possibly Clark was describing the Fortress of the Immaculate Conception (1675) east of San Carlos.

50 As difficult as this may be to read, this sentence exemplifies limited world exposure and conditions that generate bias.

51 Nicaragua has many cultures and lands of heritage represented within its 21st Century population. Sixty-nine percent of the ethnic population of Nicaragua along the west coast is "Mestizo"—Amerindian and white mix. Seventeen percent are of Spanish descent and White heritage. Five percent are indigenous Amerindian. Other sources report people with a darker complexion on the Caribbean/Atlantic side have Jamaican, West Indian, and Congo heritage, stemming from the African slave trade. CIA World Fact Book (2007), https://www.cia.gov/the-world-factbook/countries/nicaragua/.

The evening we came from San Carless to Revous, we passed through a heavy forest. The trees had a very heavy top with long drooping limbs that came over and touched near the ground. While passing this forest, we came close to a company of monkeys crossing the trail. They were of a brownish color and were tolerable [terribly] large. One of the boys began shooting their revolvers at them. Wain Oliver called to them to put up their revolvers and quit shooting. "If you do not, you will have one of the worst fights you have ever had." When the boys would shoot, the old monkeys would squall, turn, and make the most hideous faces showing their teeth at them. The young monkeys and old mammies went before us while the old men went next to us, and the way they went through that timber was funny to see. They would hook or wrap their tail on a limb, give a swing, and spring ten feet, catching with their front feet or hands. There must have been one hundred or more in this band.

Here, I saw a number of parakeets, a species of the parrot. They are a greenish color with a bright spot on the wings. They are a very noisy little fellow, and the head and beak shaped like the parrot but smaller. The early settlers of this country[52] remember when they were here, but they are extinct now.

The next day, after coming to Revous, some of our men went but to see if they could find some way by which we could cross the lake and go down the Nicaragua River. At the lake, they found a man that owned a small craft and said he thought it large enough to carry us all. He would charge us thirty dollars each for service—I think that was the price—if we furnished our own provisions. But he would have to fix seats for us, and this consumed two days. He did this by making strips fast to the gunnel or bulwarks of the vessel, putting a plank across the hull for seats.

Off to the southeast of Old Ravous, we could see the smoke and, at night, the light of a volcano, and we felt several shocks while there. As soon as our man got his boat ready, we had some provisions prepared and

---

52 Presumably, recalled by Northeast Missourians and those who emigrated there from Maryland, Virginia and Kentucky. The Carolina parakeet was once native to the plains states eastward until the early 1900s, and officially extinct as of 1939. (Birdlife International, 2023)

were ready to go. Our little sailor could not come close to shore, there being no wharf. We hired the natives there to take us in their skiffs. It would strike about the armpits if no wave struck him. While the natives were busy with the skiffs, there was a tall, slick native that had no skiff running around, wanting to carry someone in. He would kneel down and pat his shoulders for you to get on. I told Stokes Oliver that, if he would take my luggage, I would ride that native in. He gave me to understand he would take me for twenty-five cents. I gave him the quarter and mounted on his shoulders, letting my feet come down around in front. He caught around my legs with his arms, and I caught across his forehead with my hands and away we went. Natives and all stopped to look. When we got about halfway across, there came a big wave that ran clear over the native's head and wet me above the waist. What a shouting and laughing there was there. But my native kept wading and took me in pretty wet.

Our little sailboat was loaded to the guards. When we got aboard there was no room to walk around, so we sat in our seats all the time. We all got aboard and under sail about ten o'clock a.m., landing at two next day. This brings us to the Nicaragua River.[53]

It seemed that the natives had heard of us and were expecting our coming. We had to make another change in our way of traveling. We were compelled to adopt the natives' bungo or canoe to take us down the river. Those bungos are made of large logs worked out and shaped like a canoe. I cannot give the dimensions of the one I occupied, but it was a large one and carried ten Americans, six native oarsmen, and one captain who managed the rudder and other official duties. He was a fine specimen for a captain: very black, at least six feet tall, hair straight.

This country at that time was laid out in small provinces, some under Spain and some under Great Britain; consequently, in passing from one province to another, it was the duty of our captain to land the bungo then go ashore to get a passport. *We, as Americans, ought to have felt proud to be represented to the powers by that noble-looking captain.*

The river at this time was pretty high and spread over the bottoms

---

53 San Juan River

so much that, on this account. our natives could not find a suitable place to stop for the night until after dark. When we did find a place, it looked like a jungle. After tramping around, we selected a place, and the natives made a fire. They cooked them some supper, swung their hammocks to the limbs of the trees, and crawled in for the night. After sitting around the fire and nodding until midnight, we began one by one to wrap up in our blankets and lie down on the ground. Finally, I did the same but was thinking of alligators when I went to sleep. About two o'clock, it began to rain. There was one of the boys lying behind me that woke up when it began to rain. So, he started to go where the fire was, but it had burned down. It was so dark that he could not see, and as my hair was long, he stepped on it. Oh! How it pulled! I thought an alligator had me! I yelled and jumped up with my revolver in hand. He spoke and that settled it, but we had made so much fuss that we raised the camp. Then we made the natives get up and get the bungo. We got in, pulled out, and would not let them go ashore anymore—only when our captain had to. So, them natives pulled oars all day and until midnight until they became so tired and sleepy that we could not keep them awake. Seeing this, we made them get under the seats and go to sleep. Then we took the oars and made her move. When one got tired, we would change. In this way, we ran on until daybreak. We were making her get when, all at once, she gave a jerk and stood still. We got out of the current and ran on a sandbar.

We pulled and tried to push with the strike poles but could not move it, so we woke the natives and all tried [together] but could do nothing. Then, we made signs for them to get out, lift up, and push, but they refused. Some of the men drew their revolvers and shouted at them like mad people and made as though they were going to shoot them. They all jumped at the same time, some on one side and some on the other. We all helped and soon flirted her off. The natives were so afraid of alligators that you could hardly force them into the water. The natives took the oars and pulled us the rest of the way.

About nine o'clock that morning, we pulled up in front of St. George. This is—or was—under British protection as the name indicates. There was a fort there. I do not know how many days we stayed there, but we stayed several days. As I have said, there was no established line here then, but we hoped to meet a sail vessel if nothing better.

After several days, a British Steamer came in one evening with supplies for the fort, and the captain said he was going around by Panama. Our men sent word by him to the authorities, requesting to send a vessel for us; and within a few days, the steamship *Daniel Webster* came for us. We were thirty-two days from San Francisco to San Wan and twenty-one days from the time we left the ship until we took the ship on this side. The steamship ran in and anchored in the forenoon, and the captain and clerk came ashore to sell us tickets for New York, for she was on that line. But the captain said that he would stop at Havana, Cuba. We all bought tickets. I do not remember what a cab ticket cost, for it was costing us so much that Wain and Stokes Oliver and I concluded to try the steerage and bought tickets. But Stokes Oliver was sick when we got aboard and grew worse that evening. We had the doctor that morning, and he said that we had better move him into the cabin, and one of us must go with him to wait on him and give him medicine. Wain said that, if I would go as nurse, he would pay the difference and get tickets for both, so we made the exchange. By the time we got to Havana, Stokes was about well.

We had a nice run on this trip and made good time, but I do not remember how many days we were running it. At dinner, on the evening that we came to the harbor, the captain said, "Passengers, I understand that quite a number of you live in Missouri, Iowa, and the west of Illinois. I would advise you to go by the way of New Orleans and not to New York as you are just from a warm climate; it will go hard with you to stand that cold climate." But said the passengers, "We have bought tickets to New York, how about that?"

"Oh, that need not be any trouble; I will only charge you in proportion to the distance went on your tickets and pay you the money back that is due you."

So, this was agreeable, and the clerk took in our tickets and about thirty-five made the change. That night at 10 o'clock, we ran into the harbor and anchored. Next morning, the captain said he had business to attend to in the city and that, when he came back, he would bring an officer with him who would give us permits to land. When the captain returned, there were two men with him who made out permits for us and charged two dollars for each one and saying they would send boats for us to land. Captain showed us the wharf and said, "There will be two officers there who will demand your arms, and I would advise you to give them over cheerfully and do not try to conceal them. If you do and get caught, it would go hard with you."

In due time, the boats came for us, and we landed where the captain indicated. The captain had also said that our arms would be conveyed to the custom house and turned over to the American Council. When we bought tickets to depart, we went to the American Council and received our arms. As I have said, we landed where the captain said we would and found things as described. Two men met us as officers and demanded our arms, and we handed them over without a word. Here, we made a mistake. Instead of going with those officers to the Council, we trusted them to convey our arms, and we hurried off for a hotel. After dinner, a group of us boys were standing in front of the hotel when a half-Spaniard and half-American drove up in front of the hotel and asked us if we wished to take a drive out through the gate, as it was called, into the city to the waterfronts, pleasant walks, and beautiful drives. He said that he could take four comfortably and would drive us for two dollars each. So, four of us got in, and away we went a pleasure seeing.

There was no use talking; Havana was a beautiful and rich city at that time, but a part of it was badly layed out with very narrow streets. After getting out into the main city, we drove to the waterfront. This was nice. Twelve images of animals cut out of stone sat on pillars with streams of bright clear water gushing from their mouths. And the prettiest walks all strewn with the rarest sea shells, flowers and evergreens. But, oh my, with what scum we were looked upon, and it seemed like a contagion! It spread and it seemed as if the eyes of the throng were turned on us. At one time, it looked like the negroes and low tribes of the city would take us, so we ordered the driver to turn away. At one place, the driver had to force his team through. When we got through this street, we turned to the suburbs, for I felt anxious to get sight of some coffee field or to see a coffee bush. But those blacks aggravated us so much that we turned toward the main city again.

We now began to understand our situation: General Lopez Narciso,[54] a military adventurer and refuge from Havana in 1849 and 1851 planned—with the aid of Governor Quitman of Mississippi and other Southerners—the capture and annexation of Cuba. The first expedition was frustrated by President Tyler. The second, three hundred strong, landed at Cardenas and captured the town but was quickly expelled. Lopez was arrested at Savannah, but he was released for want of evidence. The third expedition landed at Las Pagas in 1851. The inhabitants fled instead of giving their aid, and the invaders were set upon by the government troops, quickly dispersing. Lopez fled to the mountains but was captured and executed at Havana September 1, 1851. I gave this from history. We landed at Havana near the middle of December 1851. It being so soon after the execution, the Spanish were hard on us.

When we returned to the hotel from our ride, it was almost sunset. Some of the boys told me that Wain Oliver left word that I would find him and Stokes at a certain hotel on a certain street. I was not going to ramble around to hunt them that night but would wait until morning. The landlord, being short of bedding and to accommodate all, made room for a lot of us by spreading blankets on the floor. We lay in rows across the room.

There was a Mr. Cannon with us, an old bachelor and a rather peculiar man. He had just two thousand dollars in gold dust. He was very fearful of losing it, so much so that we could not persuade him to deposit it on the ship or take it off at any time. He carried it in two buckskin purses, had them large so he could press them down flat then put them in a belt, one on each side, and carried them this way all the time. Being in a hot climate, he got very sore; so, that night he lay on the side row. Situated as we were that night, we ought to have kept guard in that room, for each

----

54 General Narciso López was a Native of Venezuela, who, as a teen, was forced to fight for the Spanish. He was assigned to serve as Assistant General of Cuba, over which the Spanish military had control. He became an anti-Spain revolutionary in 1848 and fled to the United States (as did many in Europe during that year of revolutions around the globe) when the Spanish began to arrest the Cuban revolutionaries. Alliances with the United States led to several military strategies to add Cuba as a slave state of the United States.

man had to keep his gold on his person. About two o'clock, Cannon raised the yell that he was robbed. We all sprung up and struck a light. Sure enough, there was one sack gone. Cannon said he was lying on his side when he awoke, and it was evident that the thief had cut through his clothing, split the belt, and lifted the sack of gold out. He never got any clue, but suspicion rested on the landlord.

By sunrise the next morning, I struck out to look for Wain and Stokes. I met them carrying our grip[55] and asked where they were going. Wain said he believed them fellows up yonder tried to get in and rob us last night. I said, "You need not go down where we were, for Cannon lost a thousand last night."

"Well, well; what will we do?"

I suggested that we try and find a French tavern. Wain caught at the idea and said, "That's right." So, we set out to find a French house. We walked for some time, not knowing where to go. Finally, we met a yellow negro, and Wain bid him good morning. And he answered back as plain as Wain. Then, Wain asked him if he knew where we could get board at a French house, where we would be treated right. He said he thought he could. Wain told him he would give him two dollars if he would take us to a good house. The first house could not take us in but told us of another that he thought would, so we went there. By hard persuasion and agreeing to let his two small children have access to our room during the day, [the landlord] consented to take us at two dollars a day. The reason he wanted the children in our room was to learn the American language. The other boys changed around, but we managed to be together some each day.

About the third or fourth day, after we got settled down and had pretty good homes, a crowd of us collected one afternoon. Amongst us was a man from Texas. He claimed to have belonged to the Texas Rangers. Let that be as it may, I know he had a couple of fine revolvers. This Texas man asked the question if we thought the American Consul would let us in the armory to rub up our knives and revolvers. The landlord said he thought he would. The Texas man said he would go if anyone would go

---

55 grip: from gripsack, a canvas or leather travel bag to hold one's belongings.

with him, so four of us went and called on the American Consul, asking him if we could be permitted to enter the armory for the purpose of cleaning our arms. He said he could by locking us in while we did the work and see that we took no arms out when we left. We consented to do as he proposed, and he then unlocked the armory and told us to walk in after showing this Texas man how to give him the signal when we wanted anything or wanted out. He stepped out and locked the door. We looked around but found none of our arms. The Texas man called for the Consul who said, "Why, what is the trouble?" We told him we could not find our arms and asked if that was all the arms he had. He said it was, then asked what our arms consisted of and how many there was. Then we told him all, where we had landed and how we delivered them to the two officers, as we thought, "with the understanding that they would be turned over to your keeping."

He said, "I never received them, and that is where you missed it. You should have come with those officers and seen them hand your arms over to me."

We then saw that we were in a fix and asked him if he could not do something for us. "Yes, if two or three of you can identify those officers," or if we would prove that the captain misinformed us, then two or three of us would stay and prosecute him when we could catch them. We could not do that, for the captain had done all he could to help us and it was a mistake of our own. We would have liked to laid eyes on those supposed officers, but we never saw them or recognized them. We lost between twenty and twenty-five new Colt revolvers along with some nice knives. We bought the greater part of them in San Francisco when we decided to come the Nicaragua route. They cost us twenty-eight dollars a piece.

The ways and customs of Havana at that time differed greatly from our own. You would of laughed to see the Nobles dressed for a morning or evening drive. The vehicles were oddly constructed and were mounted with silver and two very tall wheels. The seat was in front of the wheels. They had long shafts. The horse was hitched, so he is not close to the vehicle. I have forgotten what they call it but the fun is the way the driver and horse were rigged up. The driver was a black negro; the blacker the better, it seemed. They were dressed in a black suit with a tall black hat. The horse's mane and tail were plaited and tied with ribbons, the tail brought around to his side and tied to a ring in the shaft. The saddle was mounted with silver. This is put on the horse and the negro mounts in all his African pride, and away he goes, chug, chug, the noblemen sitting crouched back in the seat reading the morning news.

I was in a Catholic church once while in Havana. It was a rich church, a great many of the images appeared to be solid gold. And about the altar the vessels contained a large amount of gold. The Spaniards did but little work, and the negroes and creoles did the work. The negroes did the principal part of loading vessels, that is, according to my limited observation. I watched a crew one forenoon taking goods from the hole of a vessel. There was a lead; they might have called him captain. Anyway, he led the van. They were stripped to the brich. It seemed to me they went by signs and had a ying yang kind of song. The leader would start his ying yang, all singing and keeping perfect time with their bodies and hands. They would work until I could see great drops of sweat running down their backs in loading and unloading vessels; from six until eleven o'clock in the morning consisted of a day's work.

The two Olivers and I had a nice home with our old Frenchman. The fare was splendid but too dear for me to keep up long. After being there several days, one morning Wain Oliver said, when he came back from being down by the wharf, "Boys, I think there is a chance for us to get off soon for New Orleans." He had talked with the captain of a sail vessel who said he would sail for New Orleans in a day or two and could take twenty-five or thirty passengers. We had been here long enough to grow tired and disgusted and tried to get away on most anything. So a crowd of us went to see him and urged him to go. He agreed to sail some time next day.

We all felt glad to get away from that place. We had lived under Spanish rule eight days and all managed to escape the guard house. That morning the Olivers and I settled our board bill with the Frenchman and went where the other boys were. Then we all went to the wharf and the old captain took us aboard. It seems to me that we just registered and paid our fare without tickets, but what the amount was, I can't say now. It must have been near the middle of December when we landed at Havana, Cuba, for the old Captain gave us a big Christmas dinner about midway [through] the Gulf.

NEW ORLEANS TO HOME

When we came to the mouth of the Mississippi River, or where the salt water and freshwater came together, we anchored. And next morning, the tow boat hitched onto us. The boat towed three ships up to New Orleans, one lashed to each side and one behind. We had a big playground now to run over.

We landed at New Orleans at ten o'clock in the morning and went up to a hotel to register. After dinner, we bought us some new clothes, took a bath, and changed clothes. Now we felt as though we were almost home. Wain, Stokes, and I went to the United States Mint and showed our dust to the officers. I sold what dust I had for eighteen dollars an ounce. Wain had considerable dust and got the notion that we would have it coined. He would have to wait three days to have it done. He begged me so hard to stay with him that I consented. He also had Stokes put his dust in with his. I now don't see why I did not go in where they smelted and coined gold, unless it was because I had seen so much that I had got tired of seeing.

The packet pulled out for St. Louis the next morning. After we got to New Orleans, and the boys all left us, our company had got down small, only three. Although we had a long tiresome trying trip, yet we had a remarkable trip, for we had no burial at sea—only lost one man, and he was buried at New Orleans.

As the officer promised, Wain and Stokes' coin was ready the evening of the third day. The next morning, after settling our hotel bill, we started to look for a boat to St. Louis. We soon found one of those old timers that run on the lower Mississippi. She was a big old cutter with the old side wheels, and I think drew about seven foot of water. But it was the only one we could find, so we went to buy tickets. And there was only three rooms but what was taken, and one of them was over the wheelhouse. As Stokes was not well, and Wain considerably older, the wheelhouse room fell to me. This old boat was crowded both in the cabin and below.

There was a whole lot of Germans aboard going up to St. Louis, and they would waltz and dance most every night. The old captain was of the regular, old southern type and a jolly soul; and if they didn't have a gay old time, I don't know.

The first few nights I did not sleep well, for the wheel was splashing and creaking; but I soon adjusted so when it stopped, I would wake up. The river was low, and the boat would run aground most every night. When she could not pull off herself, the captain would send the cable ashore in a skiff and run it around a tree, bring the end back to the boat and rig block and tackle in some way. Then, get a whole lot of passengers and deckhands to pull and by the help of the engine, pull her off, then go on until the next time. I remember one night, she hung up about one o'clock, and they were in a big way of dancing when the captain came into the cabin and called out, "Passengers, I am aground and cannot get off without help." One big fellow yelled out, "Let her lay Captain until we get through dancing, and we will pull her off in the morning." The Captain could not get her off, so she did lay there until morning.

The Captain said he did not care to go to St. Louis before the river froze up for it was his last trip for the winter. When we got to the mouth of the Red River, we met quite a raise in the Mississippi River—and here I parted with Wain and Stokes Oliver for the last time.

I now felt quite lonely…all my California boys gone. But I had formed a partial acquaintance with an Illinoisan who had been to New Orleans with horses, and had contracted a deep cold, now sick. I turned my attention to him until we got to St. Louis.

We did not get aground after we met the rise in the river and were getting pretty well up towards St. Louis. At supper, the Captain said, "Boys, I think if we have no bad luck, by tomorrow night, we will be in St. Louis."

Next morning, when we got up, the wind was coming from the Northwest, and ice was in the river. It grew cold awful fast. The old Captain got in a bustle now and made the fireman throw the wood in the furnace. He did all he could to hurry us on. We passengers helped wood.

We all felt interested. The ice got heavier all the time, and about three o'clock the captain came in the cabin and said, "Passengers, I will have to wood fast up here and I want to take on enough to last us through; and if you will, when the plank is shot out, every man spring to it, and wood as quick as possible."

We all put on our hats and gloves and watched, and when the time came, we all ran out and loaded in a hurry. When the bell tapped, we all scud in as quickly as possible, hauled in the gang plank, and she pulled for the channel. But she never made it. A heavy body of ice struck her and she held it for some time. Finally, she gave back, and the ice pushed her against the bank on the Illinois side. We were fourteen miles below St. Louis, fast and tight. I think the boat's crew worked about all night putting in timbers to fend off the ice.

Next morning, the Captain was the same jolly old Captain and had runners out all through the neighborhood hiring wagons, buggies, sleds or anything that could carry passengers to St. Louis. It was cold that morning, or I thought so, with snow on the ground. I did not leave the boat until about ten o'clock. The sick horseman and I, with some others, went up on a sled. We paid our own fare at the ferry. Old Captain would of paid, but the men said no. By the time my sick man and I got to the hotel, it was almost dark. We put up at the old City Hotel. Next morning, my man seemed better. After breakfast, I told him that I would like to go around in the city and see if I could find a man that I thought was there. He said, "Certainly; I am all right now. This Landlord knows where I live, and I will be cared for.

Just as I got out on the sidewalk, a bus drove up in front and stopped. I called to the driver and asked if he knew a man by the name of Wiles, that at one time ran a hotel called the Wiles House. "Yes, he runs it yet. Do you want to go there? If you do, he is on this line."

I got in and was soon at Pete Wiles', the man that helped get up the mule train that I have spoken of previously and at one time lived in Monroe County, south of Hunnewell. I walked into the bar room. Pete was sitting by the stove. I recognized him at once, but of course he did not know me as I was but a boy when he last saw me. I soon let him know where I belonged. He took me right in the family room and introduced me to his wife and family, and what a time we had. His wife and I were second cousins and I almost felt at home.

The next morning Pete asked how I was going to get home. I said I guessed I would go on the stage, there being a stage route via New London and to Palmyra then. "Well," said he, "you had better go down to the stage office and register, for they are behind. So we went, and they were a week behind. *Oh, just think the way we had to travel fifty years ago. People would go mad if they had to do that way now. I was actually fourteen days coming from New Orleans to St. Louis. Now could go three times to California in the same length of time.*

I did not register on the stage line, but bought me a horse, saddle and bridle, and I came from St. Louis a-horseback. So, you see, I traveled many ways to get home but very slow ways.

There was nothing special occurred on my way home, only it was awful cold weather. There were two days that I did not travel much on account of the severe cold. I had splendid health all the way on my trip, never missed a meal when I could get it.

I arrived at father's at sunset on the 23rd of January, 1852. Left the mines October 4, 1851. Left the parental roof April 7, 1850. Arrived in California August 30, 1850.

There was great rejoicing the evening I got home, especially with mother and my sisters, for they had almost gave me up as lost. Brother Sam[56] had wrote home when I left the mines, and it had been so long that they had about give me up. But a ray of hope came to them a short time before in this way:

I had parted with a Dr. Brown of Lewis County in New Orleans who came on before me, owing to my delay there and my slow boat. And the freeze-up threw him ten days or more ahead of me. He stopped at Palmyra to visit some friends, and amongst the rest a Mrs. Shannon, who was living in Palmyra at that time but formerly in our neighborhood—in

---

56 Samuel V. Clark returned June 1853. He married Margaret Anderson, then later, after Margaret died in 1865, married her cousin Amanda (25 years his junior) with whom he had three children.

fact, father's nearest neighbor. She had heard of my delay and mother's distress, so she asked Dr. Brown if he had heard of me. But not being intimately acquainted, [he] said he did not know, but had parted with a Bob Clark at New Orleans, a man with a crippled front finger on his left hand. So, Aunt Polly Shannon sent mother this good news. Yet, my delay caused them to doubt.

Robert Clark concludes the newspaper serial with the following reflective thoughts and admonition to his readers:

While I have been living over in mind my past life, my mind caught the reflection of the spiritual for it seems to me, in some sense, that this life faintly illustrates to the Eternal. For when we feel cast down and weary with anxiety and care, trouble and sorrow and bereft, it is as an oasis in a desert land when we take in the bright promises that is held out to us in the Book of Life, then we can say with the poet,[57]

> I've found a glad hosanna, For every woe and wail,
> & handful of sweet manna, When grapes of Eschol fail,
> I've found a Rock of Ages, When desert wells are dry,
> and after weary stages I've found an Elim nigh.

It has been said the aged man who has walked with God is always ready for the Master's call, his loins are girded about and his lights burning. He lies down with the kings of the earth, and that levelling process which is thus estimated and begun in death, he feels, is the order of a higher plane of life to come.

When all the abuses and incongruities of human government will be swept away, an omniscient wisdom will shine on all alike. There will he meet the little child who strayed from the fold into the snows of death

---

57 A poem by Jane F. Crewdson, "Joy in Sorrow" from *A Little While, and Other Poems*. Manchester, England, 1864. It was set to music as a hymn by Ira D. Sankey (1840-1908). http://www.hymntime.com

early in the married life. And there will he sit beside that fond heart who heard his first piteous wail in this cold world and nestled him to her bosom warm with a mother's love. It is the one chance of happiness, and only death stands in the way. Nature carries the soul gently over the river where those who have gone before stand waiting in glad expectation.

Shall we doubt either the goodness of God or the perfection of nature, shall we hesitate to weave the silk of death around our bodies when we know that we may thence issue a being worthy of a celestial sphere of action? How we should rejoice, say Sir Robert Hall, in the prospect of spending a blissful eternity with those whom we loved on earth, of seeing them emerge from the ruins of the tomb and the deeper ruins of the fall, not only uninjured but refined and perfected with every tear wiped from their eyes. Standing before the throne of God and the lamb, in white robes and palms in their hands crying with a loud voice, "Salvation to God that sitteth upon the throne and to the lamb forever and ever." These are some of the bright promises held out to us in the Book of Life. Are we not blessed?

I now bid you good-bye.

— Robert Mason Clark

AFTERWORD

Both Robert and his brother Sam returned safely to Marion County to raise sizeable families as the "Clark Families" appendix to this compilation indicates. Robert's grand-daughter, Edna L. Clark, at age 69, wrote the following note at the end of her re-typing of Robert Clark's serial segments that appeared in the *Hunnewell Graphic* in 1903.

> Our Grandfather, Robert Mason Clark, was born October 8th, 1828 and died April 18th, 1917 at the age of 88 years, 6 months and 10 days. He wrote the foregoing account of his "Journey Across the Plains," and it was printed in serial form in the local paper, the Hunnewell Graphic, early in the 1900's. The office of the Hunnewell Graphic burned down several years ago together with their records and is no longer published. We were fortunate in obtaining copy of the published chapters from other grandchildren and thereby make up additional copies to pass on to his great-great-great-grandchildren.
>
> Edna L Clark Hoxworth, 10-4-70

A photograph of one of Hoxworth's re-typed pages—the source of this compilation—as well as a photocopy of how Clark's serial column appeared in *Hunnewell Graphic* are found in the Appendices. The photocopy of the *Hunnewell Graphic* column was made from microfilm housed in the State Historical Society of Missouri Newspaper Collection in Ellis Library on the University of Missouri-Columbia Research Center. Not all issues of the *Hunnewell Graphic* were in the SHSMO Collection; it is serendipity that some did exist beyond the burning and closing of the newspaper building in 1967.

M. K. C.

APPENDICES

A Timeline of Key Events Along the Journey

January 1850	- Sam and Bob Clark, Bill Anderson, Frank See begin discussions about going west
February	- Meet Mike Heckard, Carson Gatewood, Henley Maddox, all of North River near Palmyra, while in Quincy. These decide to travel together. Obtained oxen, other provisions in Marion County and Quincy, Illinois.
6 April	- Loaded wagon. Met Heckard, Gatewood and Maddox at Uncle Alex Anderson farm, to leave the next day.
7 April	- The seven men departed from Anderson home. Many friends traveled along as far as New Market, Missouri. Rested two miles west of Warren.
8 April	- Camped on a creek west of Shelbyville, Missouri.
9 April	- Met with seven men from Ralls County in two wagons: Dave Davenport, Jim Hagar, two Fuson boys, Tom J. Spalding, a man named Brown, and one other. Traveled to Bloomington, Macon County, where a middle-aged man wrote *Success to the Enterprising Young Men* on the Clark wagon sheet. Camped on the West side of the Chariton River bottom. At this point, there were 4 wagons, 18 oxen, 6 horses, and 4 mules.
1 May	- Began drive near St. Joseph, Missouri - At St. Joe, joined a man named Mr. Smoot and 4 men from Clark County, and 2 from Indiana. This formed a train of 7 wagons, 25 men, 64 oxen, 7 horses. Smoot was Captain. Heckard was wagon master. Parted from Ralls County "boys" at this time.

8 May	- Loaded wagons with all they could hold and ferried the Missouri River. Camped on the Missouri River bottom.
9 May	- Had snow flurries. Met a company of Indians.
13 May	- Made it to Platte Valley. Had rain storms. Drove on to Fort Kearney ("Carney") along the Platte River, in the lower middle of what is today Nebraska
date unknown	- On the Trail. Crossed the South Platte River, went up the North Platte River (still in Nebraska), and met another train - Traveled up the Platte until reaching Laramie Fork (Ft. Laramie, the SE corner of Wyoming), when the country "became rough and broken." Encountered prairie dog towns. Continued along North Platte River. - Ran the train north of the Fork. "Alkali dust and grit hurt eyes" where they donned goggles. - Met Kit Carson "the Grizzly" near Black Hills; He advised they travel by Sublette's cut-off. Carson was on his way to St. Joseph, Missouri - Began to encounter evidence of cholera. Train voted to travel on the Sabbath to avoid cholera. - Camped on a creek: Thompson's Fork, where Indians tried to stampede their stock. - Encountered ten Indians. Indian killed by ox goad while defending woman. - American Desert – 60 miles across; had to ferry across it. Met with the Ralls County wagons again. - Green River (Wyoming). Bob Clark encountered "cholera morbus" and was ill for several days.
4 July	- Devil's Pass, 200 feet or more high with many swallows. Climbed up on the crevices. Began Sweetwater River off North Platte. - Sublette's Cutoff (5 miles north of today's Fossil Butte National Monument in SW Wyoming, near Kemmerer).

date unknown   - Came to the head of the Humboldt River
(Nevada, running along today's Interstate 80).
- Hard driving, lots of sand going down the River.
Small desert with barren sandy strip five to 15 miles
across. The Humboldt Meadows (the last crossing)
"was very hard" --northwest Nevada; Alkali lakes.
- After crossing the desert on Carson Valley, grazed
for 6 days to rest near the foothills "beneath the
shade of the splendid pine forests."
- Started climbing the Sierra Nevada Mountains.

30 August   - After 4 months and 23 days, arrived in California.
Sold the teams and bought mining tools.
- Said goodbye to Heckart, Gatewood, Anderson
and Maddox, who chose to work the Feather River;
- Clarks proceeded to the South Fork of the
American River. Joined with Bob Gosney and James
Price.

date unknown   - Drove to a mining town called Weaverville [also
named Weberville,] along the American River. Met
Frank See again.
- Worked along the "McCosney" River. Here, Bob
Clark encountered severe diarrhea, preventing him
from working for over a month. [doctored with
brandy, opium, and camphor].

Winter 1850-51 - Settled for winter in Fiddletown [east of
Sacramento].

1851   - Prospected on Dry Creek, where he worked until
the middle of November. Joined a company of 40
miners, the first miners on the creek. Provided food
for the Claim by hunting.
- Built cabins in a circle, on a small valley at the
upper end where there was a small canyon. Large
American Indian town 8 miles from there.

3 October	- Rise in the river ended flume mining
4 October	- Bob Clark left after over thirteen months of mining (was ill). Prepared gold belt for the travel home with Wain and Stokes Oliver. Purchased guns and knives to take to Missouri. Sam Clark stayed in California, and mailed a letter to his family in Missouri to inform them Bob was on his way back home.
Mid-October	- Bob and Olivers departed for Pacific Ocean voyage to Missouri. Sailed on a -mast vessel, *The Lowell*, holding 65 passengers. Tremendous storm. Harpooned shark, saw whale and porpoises.
November	- Arrived at "San Carless" and "Revous" (Rivas). Crossed Lake Nicaragua.
	- Passed through heavy forest. Crossed monkey trail: over 100 monkeys "brownish and tolerable large" and parakeets prevailed.
	- Crossed lake and cruised Nicaragua River on a little sail boat. Came to a British Fort: St. George. Took steamer *Daniel Webster* bound for St. Louis and New York Exited at Havana, Cuba.
December	- Celebrated Christmas while crossing the Gulf of Mexico
	- Stayed about a week in Havana, Cuba, where Bob Clark lost his diary. Bob along with Wain and Stokes Oliver were robbed of 25 Colt revolvers and some high-quality knives they purchased in San Francisco. Transferred to a boat going to New Orleans.
1852	
January	- Took an "old cutter with side wheels" bound up the Mississippi. Traveled with many German emigrants on board, also going to St. Louis.
	- A rise in the Mississippi at the Red River; Here,

Wain and Stokes Oliver separated from Robert Clark.
-   14 miles below reaching St. Louis (probably near
Columbia, IL), ice pushed the cutter to bank on the
Illinois side. The passengers took sleds and then a
ferry (possibly the Piggott Ferry) to reach St. Louis.
Stayed at "Old City Hotel." Located Peter Wiles in
St. Louis, and visited in his lodging house. Wiles was
formerly of Monroe County, MO.
-   Robert Clark bought a horse, saddle and bridle
from Wiles, and rode in cold weather from St. Louis
on horseback.

23 January   -   Robert Clark arrived at his parents' home at sunset.

Mining Sites Worked by Robert Clark

words in italics are phrases from the memoir

August 30, 1850 Arrived in California

WEAVERVILLE – near the McCosney River[58] (McCosmer/ McCosmey—various spellings)

The first drive/stop mentioned after arriving in California. The six from Marion County who initially mined together included Mike Heckard, Carson Gateswood, Henley Maddox, Bill Anderson, Sam Clark, and Bob Clark. Here, the Clarks reunited with Frank See.

Bob Clark and Bill Anderson prospected on "the river" that was low and barely running –*more like a creek*. Went down river until passing all other miners. Stopped at a *dry gulch or ravine where the water in time had cut a considerable ditch*. A short time after this, Bill and Bob moved down the McCosney. Sam and Mike *went down river several miles*.

---

58   Near Fiddletown, in Amador County, are the *Mokelumne* River and the Cosumnes River—and these run in El Dorado County—where the Sutter's Mill and mother lode of gold were. Fiddletown and these rivers are east of Sacramento. According to an 1850 book by Bayard Taylor, El Dorado, page 172, Cosumne River was pronounced by most as "Mokosume" with accent on the last e, as "ee". So, it is apparent McCosney River refers to the Cosumne River. This is relayed by correspondence with Elaine Zorbas, historian for Fiddletown and Amador County. Zorbas notes below Placerville–a town in El Dorado County on route 50–is Weber Creek, which was called Weaver's Creek. A mining camp called Weaverville/Weberville was along Weaver's Creek. Maps of 1848 and 1851 note "Weber" as the spelling. The Placerville settlement was once called Dry Diggins and then Hangtown before Methodist Episcopal settlers requested a more temperate name. Weberville was named after Charles Weber, a gold miner at the site in 1848, and who founded Stockton. Weber Creek is about 230 miles from Humboldt Sink. (M.M. Gordon, *Overland to California*, Stanford University Press, 1983)

Mid-October 1850
FIDDLETOWN – Selected a place for Winter where they built a cabin about seven miles from where we were and *about four miles from a little mining town called Fiddletown.*"

Mid-November 1850
DRY CREEK – met men setting up a prospecting company to go *eight miles southeast of town* to prospect on a creek called Dry Creek. Company of 40 men. Made a record, set up by-laws, staked claims on a small valley. All but the six men from Missouri were *from the East* (of the United States). The Clarks provided food by hunting, the only men who had the skills and experience.

DRY CREEK CANYON – A small canyon at the upper end of the valley where they prospected

Spring 1851
75 MILES[59] -- Sold all tools and guns and walked to the city which was called "75 Miles." Here, they split with the other Missourians. Sam and Bob went to the South Fork of the American River while others went up the Feather River. Met Bob Gosney of Marion County, Missouri. Travelled the American River to a place called Barnes Barr.

BARNES BARR[60]
James Price of Jackson County, MO launched a provision store. Sam and Bob took Wain Oliver's provisions from James River with a team and wagons, and traversed four days hauling sixty-foot logs.

---

59 Sacramento is about 50 miles from Fiddletown

60 Barnes Bar is along the North Fork of the American River, according to several gold rush accounts, including *The History of the North Fork of the American River.* Towle, Russell. (https://www.northforktrails.com/)

May 8, 1851
OLIVER-KIBBY CLAIMS – Worked the Oliver Claim with Wain Oliver and Stokes Oliver It was situated below the Kibby Claim, both claims comprised of men from Jackson County. The men of the two claims collaborated, working equally along the creek, fourteen hands. Made a dam to run two flumes, uncovering several hundred dollars of gold per day.

Oct 4, 1851 Departed mine fields for return to Missouri
Robert Clark, becoming weaker in health, left the mines. He travelled with the Olivers to San Francisco to embark for Missouri by ship, through Nicaragua to Cuba, then north on the Mississippi River. He arrived at his Marion County home at sunset, January 23, 1852.

Map of Missouri Counties

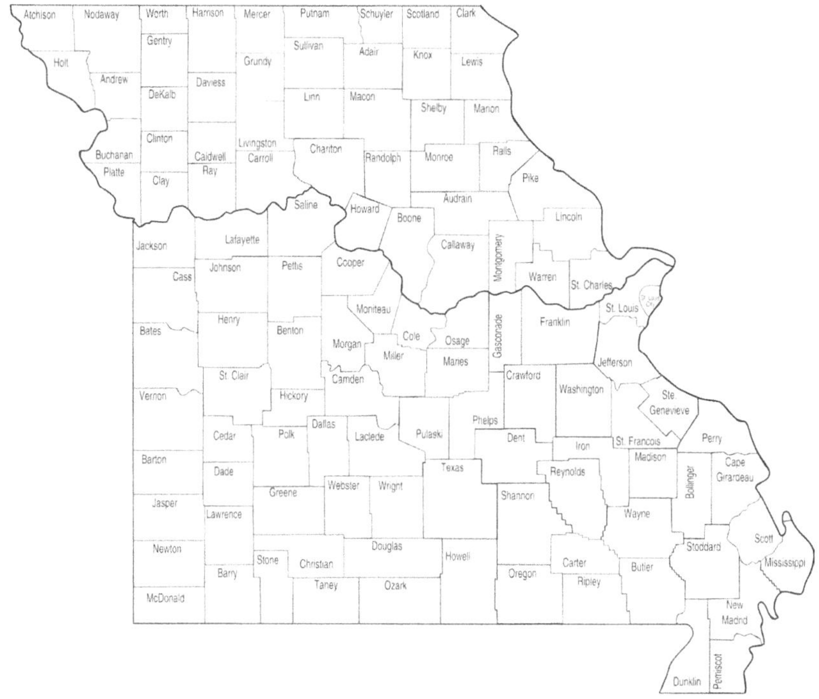

Map courtesy of Missouri State Archives, Publications Division;
Office of the Secretary of State

Counties of Northeast Missouri

Ralls County - Organized November 16, 1820, (effective January 1, 1821) from Pike

Statehood of Missouri was granted in 1821

Marion County - Organized December 23, 1826, from Ralls County
Monroe County - Organized January 6, 1831, from Ralls County
Lewis County - Organized January 2, 1833, from Marion County
Shelby County - Organized January 2, 1835, from Marion County
Clark County - Organized December 16, 1836, from Lewis County
Macon County - Organized January 6, 1837, from Randolph County
    and Chariton County
Mercer County - Organized February 14, 1845, from Grundy County

Map of
Marion County Townships

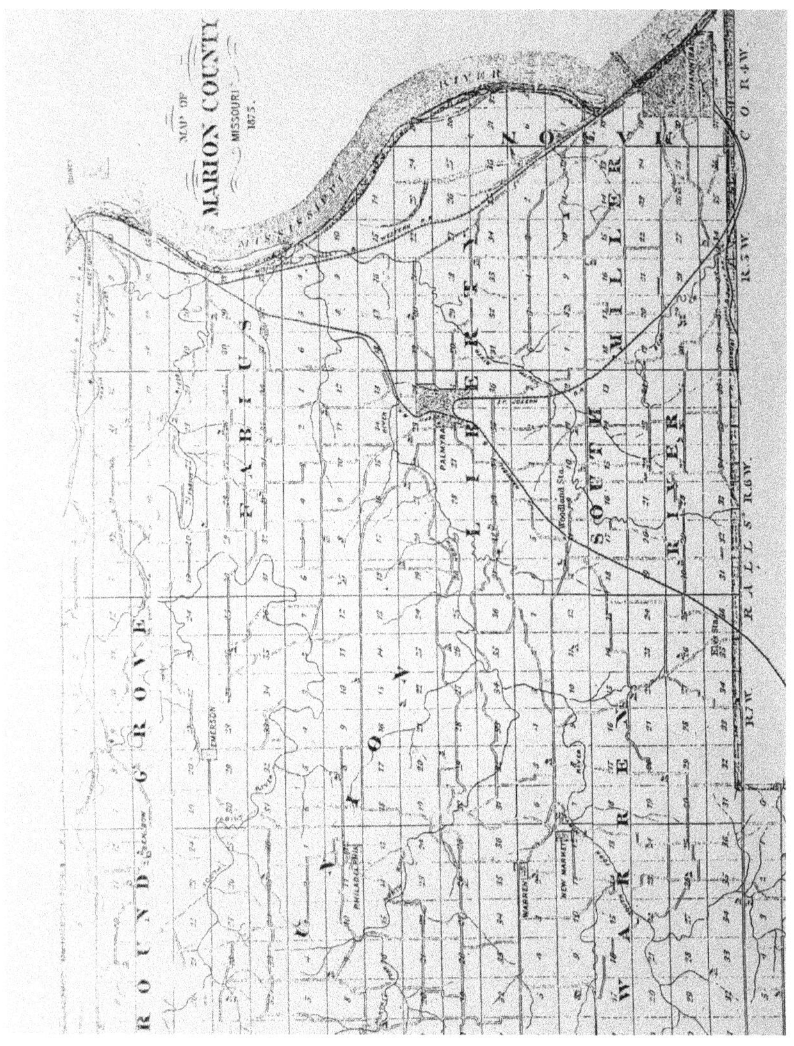

Map Atlas of Marion County, Missouri; T. M. Rogers, Quincy, Illinois, 1875

People Mentioned in Clark's Memoir Biographical Information

The Six Main Travelers from Marion County[61]

Robert Mason Clark - Also goes by "Bob." Born in Mason County, Kentucky, on October 8, 1828 and died near Hunnewell, Shelby County, Missouri April 18, 1917, at the age of more than 88 years. Son of James and Polly (Vanschoiacke) Clark, whose family moved with the Vanschoiacke family from Mason County, Kentucky to Lewis County (Warren Township), Missouri in 1830—3 years before Lewis was organized as a county.[62] Was 21 when he embarked on the journey. He married Sarah Jane Gosney on 27 Oct 1853 in Marion County.

---

61 Marion County is adjacent to Shelby County on the east, with Hunnewell sitting in Shelby close to that border. Ralls County is below Marion County, and Monroe County is below Shelby County. Jackson County is near Kansas City. Lewis and Clark Counties are near Keokuk Iowa.

62 In R.M. Clark's *The Genealogy of our Parentage*, Vanshoiacke is written with an e and lower case s.

Samuel Vanschoaick Clark - Born 5 February 1827 in Kentucky and died 15 November 1899 of typhoid at 72 years. Buried on farm near Palmyra. Sam, the older brother of Robert M. Clark, was 23 when departing for the journey. Upon return, Sam married Margaret Anderson, who died without children. Sam married her cousin Amanda Anderson, by whom he was father to offspring James, Clem, and Polly.

Frank See - Along with Bill Anderson, Sam and Robert Clark, in 1850 started scheming going to the gold region "in quest of our fortunes." Frank parted just before going over the mountains to begin mining. Reconnected at Weaverville, California, where he worked with different mining group.

Henley Maddox - Lived in North River north of Palmyra and below the Fabius River, Marion County, Missouri. Met Sam and Bill in Quincy, Illinois before trip

Carson Gatewood - Lived in North River north of Palmyra and below the Fabius River, Marion County, Missouri. Met Sam and Bill in Quincy, Illinois before trip.

Mike Heckard - Lived in North River in Fabius Township, Marion County. With Gatewood and Maddox, met Sam and Bill in Quincy Illinois. Mike was named wagon master in train of 7 wagons, 25 men, 64

Additional Missourians Met Along the Adventure

Wain Oliver, Stokes Oliver, Boutwell Oliver, James Price of Jackson County, Missouri. The Olivers set up a claim in California. **Alf Henson**, Price's half-brother.

Mr. Smoot – Of Lewis County, Missouri; no first name given; believed to be Middleton Smoot, for whom the Smoot Landing two miles south of Canton, Missouri, along the Mississippi, is named (the Smoots are from Scotland and settled in Virginia before traveling to Mason County, Kentucky).

William "Bill" Anderson - Presumably a nephew of Alex Anderson and related to the lawyer and Congressman Thomas Anderson (Andersen) and a cousin to Clarks.

Dave Davenport, Jim Hagar, 2 **Fuson** boys, a boy named **Brown** - from Clark County; another from Ralls County.

Other Key Missourians Mentioned

Alex "Uncle Alex" Anderson - Provided funds so that Robert could go on the trip with his brother Sam and Bill Anderson. (Samuel Clark m. Margaret Anderson; this could be her uncle)

Spotswood Williams - From Marion County, who crossed the plains in 1849 and sent letters back to Marion County to report aspects of his adventures and the land he traveled.

Kibby Claim - A mining claim set up above Robert Clark's team in California. The Kibby family was from Jackson County, Missouri.

Peter Wiles - Formerly of Monroe County, living in St. Louis by 1852. Boarding house and livery operator, at 108 & 110 N. 5th Street in St. Louis (per Kennedy's 1860 St. Louis City directory); which would be the block north of the Old Courthouse today (Broadway and Chestnut). Supported Robert Clark upon his return. With a Mr. Bennett, Wiles led a (failed) wagon train across the plains in 1850 — *"I think their mules were too young for the trip, and probably drove too hard" (Robert Clark)*

Dr. Brown - From Lewis County, who gave an account to a former neighbor of the Clark family [Aunt Polly Shannon, residing in Palmyra] of meeting a Bob Clark while in New Orleans, bringing good news to Bob's worried mother.

James Price - Jackson County, who had traveled west in 1849. Acquaintance of Olivers and Bob Gosney. He sold provisions; wanted to start store at Barnes Barr; asked Clarks and Gosney to help while mining near Dry Creek

Uncle Billey Moss - Sold yoke of oxen to Alex Anderson to equip the Clark lads for the trip.

Robert and Samuel Clark Families

The children of **Robert Mason Clark** (b. 8 October 1828, d. 18 April 1917) and wife **Sarah Jane (Gosney) Clark** (b.23 Sep 1828, d. 28 Jan 1905) numbered twelve, as reported in the "Genealogy of Our Parentage." This type-set booklet was prepared by Robert Mason Clark, using the information given from his father to Robert (and Samuel's) brother Dr. J. D. Clark, whose wife Jessie VanSchoiacke Clark wrote out the details by hand. Robert added additional information about offspring as he knew it. From this document and additional information gathered from sources found via online and library collections, the following is known about Robert and Sam's offspring. Names in italics indicate those not reaching adulthood.

James David Clark   b. 15 Aug. 1854 in Shelby County, Missouri; d. 8 Dec 1933
Married Louisa **Hagar** in Fall 1878; Ralls County, Missouri; d. 1 Dec. 1933, Buffalo, Wyoming

Sarah Elizabeth Clark   b. 31 Jan. 1856 in Marion County, Missouri
Married John W. **Hagar**: d. 5 Mar. 1937

Emma Jane Clark   *b. 27 Apr. 1860 in Mercer County, Missouri*
d. 15 Aug. 1860

Robert Alexander Clark   b. 25 Sept. 1861 in Mercer County, Missouri;
d. 24 Feb. 1927
Married Rachel Margaret **Baker** of Illinois on 13 January 1886

Mary Francis Clark   b. 8 Jun. 1858 in Mercer County, Missouri;
                             d. 18 Dec. 1876 in Marion County, Missouri

AryAnn Clark   *b. 22 Jun. 1857 in Mercer County, Missouri*
                             d. 8 Sept. 1857

Laura Bell Clark   *b. 27 Jun. 1866*
                             d. 7 Sept. 1867

Samuel Wilson Clark   b. 30 Dec. 1868 in Marion County, Missouri;
                             d. 25 May 1948
                             Married Helen ("Birdie") Marsh **Baird**,
                             b. 4 Apr. 1878 in Shelby County, m 12 Jan.
                             1893 in Shelbina, Missouri

Ollie Bell Clark   b. 25 Aug. 1869 in Marion County, Missouri;
                             d. 10 Oct. 1936

Lenora Clark   *b. 16 Mar. 1875;*
                             d. 18 Jul. 1876

         2 additional daughters who died young

Robert's brother **Samuel VanSchoiack Clark** (b. 5 Feb 1827, Mason County KY, d. 15 Nov 1899). He returned to Missouri in June 1853. On 27 Sept 1853 he married **Margaret J. Anderson** (b. 9 Dec 1828, d. 29 Aug 1865) on their farm in Liberty Township near Palmyra. After her death, he married **Amanda Anderson** (Margaret's cousin, 23 years younger to Sam), who bore three children: James, Clemmy and Polly. The 1880 census notes that his mother-in-law, Nancy [Ellen Watkins] Anderson, resided with them as did William Anderson, age 26—assumably, Amanda's brother. They were of the Presbyterian faith. Sam died of typhoid and was buried in the Crane Cemetery, Marion County, Missouri, next to his first wife, Margaret.

James Samuel Clark	b. Feb, 1878, Palmyra, Marion County, Missouri d. 17 March 1925, Multnomah County, Oregon
Pauline Ellen [Polly] Clark	b. 18 Oct 1879, Palmyra, Marion County, Missouri m. 28 Dec 1898, Jasper Talcott **Stillions**, Palmyra; 4 children d. 1957 Seaside, Clatsop County, Oregon (offspring residing in California)
Clem Watkins Clark	b. 17 April 1884, Palmyra, Marion County, Missouri; d. 10 Sept. 1951, Los Angeles, Los Angeles County, California

A Sample of Edna (Clark) Hoxworth's Formatting

Page 18 (eighteen)

and TIRED THAT HE WAS NOT ABLE TO GO IN THE TEAM. WE HITCHED ONE YOKE OF
HECKARD'S WITH OURS AND LED THE ODD OX BEHIND THE WAGON, AND TOLD FRANK SEE TO
TAKE THE MARE ON THROUGH TO WATER. BROTHER SAM SAID HE WOULD TRY AND BRING
THE BROKE DOWN OX ON SO HE FILLED HIS CANTEEN AND WAITED FOR THE OX TO REST,
LEAVING BILL AND I TO TAKE CARE OF THE TEAM. AT DAYLIGHT WE STOPPED AGAIN AND
GAVE THE LAST OF OUR FEED AND WATER TO THE OXEN, MADE SOME COFFEE AND HAD A KI
LITTLE BREAKFAST AND PULLED OUT ON OUR LAST DRIVE. AT NINE O'CLOCK THE SAND WA
GETTING HOT AND ALL THE BOYS GONE BUT THE DRIVER. MIKE HECKARD HAD GONE ON
TO SAVE HIS HORSE. BILL ANDERSON AND HENLY MADDOX HAD LEFT AND AS GATEWOOD
AND I WERE ON DRIVE WE HAD TO STAY FROM NINE TO TEN O'CLOCK. WE WERE MAKING
SHORT DRIVES AS THE TEAMS WOULD PULL UP A QUARTER TO A HALF A MILE AND STOP.
THE SUN AND SAND WAS SO HOT THAT SOMEONE PROPOSED TO LEAVE THE WAGONS AND
COME AND GET THEM WHEN THE SUN GOT LOW BUT NO ONE FELT WILLING TO SIT THERE
ALL DAY AND WATCH THE PROVISION. WHILST WE THUS PARLAYED, OUR CATTLE RAISED
THEIR HEADS AND STOOD A MINUTE LIKE SNIFFING THE AIR AND THEN MOVED UP AND
DID NOT STOP ON THEIR OWN A CCORD THE REST OF THE WAY. WE WERE NEAR TWO MILES
AWAY WHEN WE CLAIMED THEY SCENTED THE WATER, SO WE PULLED OVER AND CAME TO A
BEAUTIFUL STREAM CALLED SWEET WATER, OR THAT IS WHAT THE EMIGRANTS CALLED IT,
AT ABOUT LL O'CLOCK. SAM DID NOT GET IN UNTIL NEAR ONE O'CLOCK BUT HE HAD TO
LEAVE THE OX ABOUT SIX MILES BACK ON THE DESERT. SAM SAID THE OX WAS GETTING
WEAK AND AS HE WAS PASSING A DESERTED WAGON NEAR THE TRAIL, WHEN THE OX STRUCK
THE SHADE OF THE WAGON, HE DROPPED DOWN AND HE COULD NOT GET HIM UP ANY MORE.
THE WATER IN SAM'S CANTEEN HAD GIVEN OUT AND HE WAS BECOMING VERY THIRSTY. JU
BEYOND THE DESERT THE MORMONS KEPT A TRADING POST. ALSO THERE WERE TWO MEN
THAT HAULED WATER ON THE DESERT TO SELL TO THE EMIGRANTS. AS SAM CAME IN HE
MET THOSE MEN AND GAVE THEM 25 CENTS FOR A DRINK. BILL ANDERSON AND I THOUGHT
OF GOING AFTER NIGHT AND TRY TO BRING THE OX IN BUT WE WAS SO TIRED WE
CONCLUDED TO WAIT UNTIL EARLY IN THE MORNING. THAT EVENING WHILE NEAR THE
I SUT ON HERD AND FEELING WEARY I SAT DOWN ON A KNOLL. BY MOONLIGHT ONE
VALLY. I COULD SEE A SURE ENOUGH STREAM OF WATER GOING RIGHT BY MY THROUGH THE

Edna (Clark) Hoxworth's formatting of Robert Mason Clark's columns
that appeared as a serial in the *Hunnewell Graphic* during 1903

Sample of R.M. Clark's column Hunnewell Graphic

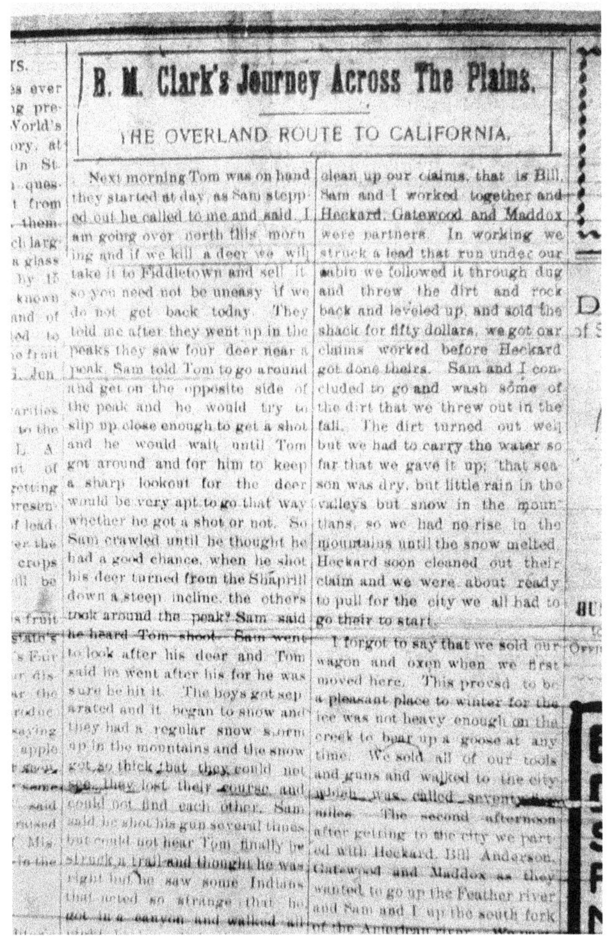

B. M. Clark's Journey Across The Plains.

THE OVERLAND ROUTE TO CALIFORNIA.

Next morning Tom was on hand they started at day, as Sam stepped out he called to me and said I am going over north this morning and if we kill a deer we will take it to Fiddletown and sell it so you need not be uneasy if we do not get back today. They told me after they went up in the peaks they saw four deer near a peak. Sam told Tom to go around and get on the opposite side of the peak and he would try to slip up close enough to get a shot and he would wait until Tom got around and for him to keep a sharp lookout for the deer would be very apt to go that way whether he got a shot or not. So Sam crawled until he thought he had a good chance, when he shot his deer turned from the Shaprill down a steep incline, the others took around the peak? Sam said he heard Tom shoot. Sam went to look after his deer and Tom said he went after his for he was sure he hit it. The boys got separated and it began to snow and they had a regular snow storm up in the mountains and the snow got so thick that they could not see, they lost their course and could not find each other. Sam said he shot his gun several times but could not hear Tom finally he struck a trail and thought he was right but he saw some Indians that acted so strange that he got in a canyon and walked all

clean up our claims, that is Bill. Sam and I worked together and Heckard, Gatewood and Maddox were partners. In working we struck a lead that run under our cabin we followed it through dug and threw the dirt and rock back and leveled up, and sold the shack for fifty dollars, we got our claims worked before Heckard got done theirs. Sam and I concluded to go and wash some of the dirt that we threw out in the fall. The dirt turned out well but we had to carry the water so far that we gave it up; that season was dry, but little rain in the valleys but snow in the mountains, so we had no rise in the mountains until the snow melted. Heckard soon cleaned out their claim and we were about ready to pull for the city we all had to go their to start.

I forgot to say that we sold our wagon and oxen when we first moved here. This proved to be a pleasant place to winter for the ice was not heavy enough on the creek to bear up a goose at any time. We sold all of our tools and guns and walked to the city which was called seventy miles. The second afternoon after getting to the city we parted with Heckard, Bill Anderson, Gatewood and Maddox as they wanted to go up the Feather river and Sam and I up the south fork of the American river.

courtesy of State Historical Society of Missouri - Columbia Center

Spotswood Williams Letters [63]

The following letter was published in the *Missouri Whig*, Palmyra, Missouri, in January, 1850. This may be the very letter that inspired the Clarks and friends to head west as Clark mentioned reading them, finding them inspirational.

—

October 7, 1849. The last *Paris Mercury* published several California letters, from which we make liberal extracts. The following dated "California Mines, Oct. 7," is from Mr. **S. S. Williams**, who went from this county last spring, to his brother, **A. G. Williams**, of Monroe County:

I have written some three letters to you since my arrival here, but supposing there is some uncertainty in the mails, I again write you, giving the time of our arrival here, as well as some description of the country and mines. We left St Joseph on the 3d day of May, and arrived in the gold diggings on the 10th of August, and reached Sacramento Valley on the 12th of the same month.

After resting ourselves and stock some two days, we started for the diggings, at which place we arrived the 25th of August. My first work was to make two cradles for washing out gold, which are simply such as are used in the States to quiet children, except that the foot end is open, with some boards

———————————+———————————

63 *The Marion County 49ers* - Letters. Collected by Kenneth E. Weant, 2004. Held at the State Historical Society of Missouri, Columbia Research Center, and at the Hannibal Public Library, Hannibal, Missouri

across the bottom, against which the gold washes, while the sand, gravel and clay, pass off. There is also a hopper on the head of the cradle, the bottom of which is sheet iron, copper or zinc, with holes for the gold, sand, &c, to pass through. This, with a pan, is all the machinery necessary to separate the gold from the gravel, sand and clay. I made those cradles in two days, and sold one of them the day after for $40. I was then taken sick, and was not able to work for near two weeks. Since which time I have been mining, and have averaged over $50 per day for the last four weeks. I expect to work at the same place some two weeks yet, after which I intend to go into the dry diggings, of to Sacramento City, and go to carpentering at an ounce a day, which I am told can easily be obtained.

I will now endeavor to give you some description of the country and mines. The rivers run through deep canons, or hills, which are from four to six hundred feet high, and so very steep as to render it impossible for man or beast to pass over them. The gold is found in the bars of gravel and sand that are deposited at the water's edge, and is generally from three to ten feet under the surface, the most of which is on the bed or bottom rock, many times five feet under the surface of the water in the river, making it very difficult to obtain, in consequence of having to fail out the water. We have occupied just such a situation for the last four weeks, requiring six hands to bail out the water, while two or three others would throw out dirt, which is very rich, yielding from $2 to $3.50 to one and a half gallons of dirt. Two hands have thrown out dirt enough in one day to make $1,450, which we washed out the next day before dinner. There were only four hands employed at this time, the water not running in as fast as it has since done. The greatest deposits of gold are supposed to be in the bed of the rivers, in the deepest holes of water, many of which are very deep. The rivers are dammed and turned in many places, where there are ripples, and the bed worked out, which, in many instances, yield a great quantity of gold, while others yield little or none. There is another species of diggings, called dry diggings, which are worked during the wet season, or winter and spring. These are situated in the ravines, that are entirely dry at this time; though we will have plenty of water for gold washing after the 20th of November. The gold in these diggings is of a much coarser quality than the river gold, (a sample of each I will send in this letter;) here the lumps of gold are found, the largest I have seen containing $126. Many persons have worked during the summer and fall in the dry diggings, some packing their dirt on mules to water to wash out the gold, and others throwing it in piles, calculating to wash it out when the rains commence. Some of the largest amounts are raised here in the dry diggings; yet men that will work can obtain one ounce, or $16 per day, in any of the mines that I have yet seen—though many with tender hands are wandering up and down these rivers, abusing the country and the mines, and many others will return to the States as soon as they get means enough for that purpose.

In relation to the emigration this year, I think there is not over one half of them have yet reached California, though many have turned to Oregon in consequence of feed for their stock the grass being entirely consumed on every route to California. Gov. Smith of California, fitted out a company of men, with pack mules, which left Sacramento City some two weeks past for the relief of emigrants. I have no information of **Heckarts** or **Kirklands**, and think they have not yet reached the mines. **Lasley**, **Hawkins** and others, reached the mines some 6 or 8 days after we did, though I know of no others from Marion county having arrived. Most persons coming across the plains, after reaching the mines, have a slight spell of sickness; but at this time I think it remarkably healthy. Miners have rough living, provision plenty, done up in our own way, with beds on the gravel and sand, and that frequently on ground so steep that you could slip out at the foot of it if you were not almost constantly crawling up towards the head. The hills frequently approach the river so near that a situation cannot be got level and large enough to stretch a tent of make a bed. In relation to returning to the States, I cannot now say at which time I will return, though I think it will be one year from next March or April. The opportunities for sending letters from here are but once a month, and I expect to embrace every opportunity to write to some of my friends in the States.

≋

An additional Letter in the Weant collection from March 10, 1850, writer unknown, mentioning Williams.[64]

I assisted in the painful duty of consigning to the grave, the past week, the remains of **John J. Hawkins**, of Hannibal, and **John Sharp**, son of my old and respected friend, **Richard Sharp**, of Marion county. They both suffered a protracted illness. **Spottswood Williams**, the brother-in-law of John Sharp has been absent sometime, and I fear is sick, or he would have been here to wait on his brother-in-law. Please drop a line to Mr. Sharp, informing him of his son's death--that he died on the 8th instant, at 9 o'clock, P. M.; that he lay sick at Mr. **Packwood**'s and that the last sad offices were performed for him by Missourians in a decent and respectful manner.

---

64 The 1860 U.S. Census [M653 roll 632, p. 686] indicates a Spot S. Williams, age 58, born in Virginia, living in South River Township of Marion County, Missouri, with his wife and seven offspring, the youngest being 8.

Segments of a Wagon Train Company's Articles of Agreement

The Following Points were in an agreement[65] drafted by Thomas L. Anderson to the specific interests of William Muldrow,[66] who formed a "Joint Stock Association" *for the purpose of an expedition to the Territory of California with the reasonable hope and expectation of improving our condition and circumstances in life by the procurement of a portion of the precious metals that are said to abound in that country.* After many words of praise for the adventurers, the Articles (abbreviated below) would appear, and the document signed by persons instrumental in its formation and leadership. One can assume the Agreement signed by the Clarks and fellow miners stipulated similar conditions.

1. All members bear an equal expense of fitting out the expedition; William Muldrow and Thomas L. Anderson are to procure everything necessary except clothing, weapons, blankets which each member is to procure for himself. Failure to pay his portion of the outfitting expense means forfeit of partnership in the Association.

---

65 Among other sources, this document is in the collection of the State Historical Society of Missouri Research Center–Columbia. Item 64 of A1177; CO995 Transcript Collection.

66 The party, led by William Muldrow, left 17 April 1849 from Philadelphia, Marion County. Muldrow soon abandoned the "share alike" concept, finding business opportunities along the way, and turned the company over to Robert Crane. Muldrow pursued wealth in many ways, from advancing Marion County as an area for a major port to doing business with Johann Sutter of Sutter's Mill in California, buying land in the Russian River valley in California, and struggling with the Russian Fur company for title to it; alas returned to Missouri a broke man in 1869. He did not pan for gold, but pursued real estate opportunities and speculated in claims.

2. All partners shall share equally in all losses or profits.

3. The Company is to continue for two years from 1 April 1849 and shall not be interfered with as to its purpose except with consent of all partners.

4. It shall continue three years leaving it optionary for partners to withdraw after two years if they give the others three months notice.

5. All partners shall go with the company and during its existence no partner is to enter into a similar agreement with another expedition.

6. If any member die or become too sick to work, he or his heirs shall share equally in the profits of the expedition for the first two years; if he fails to supply a good hand to do his work, the company shall charge him or his estate $18 a month.

7. The majority of the Company shall have the power to incur expenses or obtain leases, etc.

8. Any two members can demand a division of profits on hand any time the Company has $10,000 in the treasury, but the whole fund must be sent to Palmyra to a selected person, to distribute it equally.

9. Expedition members who reach California should be a majority decide how the gold and silver shall be kept, or taken back to Palmyra.

10. There shall be a secretary to keep a true account of all the Company's affairs.

11. One person shall be selected as manager, whose orders shall be obeyed.

12. Thomas L. Anderson[67] shall not be required to accompany the expedition; if he sends his negro man, Sandy, in his place; Sandy shall not be required to do more work than any of the partners.

13. Dr. Albert G. Anderson shall furnish a good hand, or they will

---

67 Dr. Anderson did go. He died 4 November 1840 in California. Others of that Company died as well. (Bacon, T. H.; Holcombe, R. I.)

deduct from his share $18 a month, if he does not go. If he goes, his medical services and work as a chemist shall be his share of the work, and all services he renders shall be for the Company and no other.

14.   Upon reaching California, all matters shall be governed by a majority of members present at meetings.

15.   The Company shall be known by the name and style of William Muldrow and company.

16.   This company shall neither work nor travel on the Sabbath, no member shall drink intoxicants or gamble; any member violating this article forfeits his membership in the Company.

17.   The expedition shall leave on or before the first day of April, 1849.

Enterprising Northeast Missourians
Early Influences

Compiled by Marsha K. Clark

In addition to the comments about cultural influences found in the Introduction of this book, it is worth noting the heritage of adventure that inspired argonauts on their westward pursuits in the 19th century. The following provides some accounts of how the Northeast Missouri wilderness—specifically, what became Marion, Ralls and Shelby counties—yielded to early settlement and trade, both with and without interaction of first nations who held that land along the great rivers for centuries prior.

Accounts of the families from Kentucky who migrated to the upper Louisiana Territory shed light on the challenges of those earlier days. They offer a foundation for understanding the fortitude and ambitions that eventually attracted nearly a third of the Northeast Missouri men to join the worldwide rush to pursue their dreams of gold. It is in the shadows of these accounts that the gold rush adventurers inherited a legacy for living off the land, developed an ambitious spirit, became courageous, and pursued dangerous journeys.[68]

The following narrative suggests some of the events and conditions that may have impacted the character, culture, and motivations of those who continued westward migration. It serves as prompts for continued pondering about our earliest Anglo settlers, their relations with Native

---

68 (Holcombe) Many gold rush journey accounts can be found in *History of Marion County, Missouri. St. Louis* (E.F. Perkins, 1884). Additional online sources offer hundreds of stories about California and other state mining endeavors, camps, and trails. See the bibliography for resources that include maps and other historical detail.

Americans then and now, biases of any sort, work ethic, family dynamics, and a larger social schema. Most of this information is based on secondary sources.

Launching the American Dream from the Atlantic to the Mississippi

The early American settlers who migrated into the Midwest and beyond were usually English, Scot, and Irish, or Scot-Irish, who took advantage of land grants (bounty-land warrants) released after the Revolutionary War and the War of 1812.

In 1779, an ordinance was decreed that the warranted land—known as the *Western Reserves*—would be awarded to soldiers and sailors for their service in the military efforts engaged within the young country. Parcels of land were also sold to ambitious tradesmen and those yearning for opportunity. These actions not only served to expand the new American federation but also restored the federal treasury that was indebted by war expenses. These lands encompassed what is today Kentucky and Ohio—then a part of Virginia. The bounty-land warrants following the War of 1812 were awarded only in sections of Arkansas, Illinois, Michigan, and Missouri until 1842, when other provisions for westward settlement were made by acts of Congress. The Western Reserves sold for only $1 per acre.[69] Another attractive reason for relocating west was the land ordinance's provision that the settled areas would eventually become states once the required threshold of population was attained; thus, the wild would become civilized.

Thomas Jefferson proposed the Western Reserves be divided into townships of thirty-six miles, each with one-square-mile sections comprised of 640 acres. This surveying of land into grids of *township* and *range* numbers

---

69 Most of the land grants were awarded to corporations or developers, not directly to individuals.

was used across the midwestern and western states in subsequent years as the country quickly expanded its presence and manifest authority within the Louisiana Territory. This process was not an easy endeavor. There were many trials that aspiration alone could not overcome.

Daniel Boone—famed frontier soldier and surveyor of Virginia (and of Kentucky beginning in 1769)—had skills to successfully lead hundreds of people into the upper Spanish Louisiana territory of Missouri, where he established a home in 1799 and in 1820 died in St. Charles County at age eighty-five.[70] Boone had been part of a company that established a trail through the Cumberland Gap into Kentucky and Tennessee, which became the Wilderness Road. He also used the Ohio River to assist those in the New England states relocate to Kentucky. Historical accounts suggest more than 200,000 people were brought to Kentucky under Boone's service.[71]

Kentucky became a state in 1792, the state of Virginia having ceded that portion of its land so that the financial debt incurred by the young nation during its nearly decade-long battle for independence might finally be settled. Kentucky land was for sale, and the development of the Upper Mississippi soon followed.

---

70 "Daniel Boone," Wikipedia Foundation, accessed 2023.-2024. He had accumulated debts from failed business ventures, including real estate in Mason County, Kentucky. It is suggested he took refuge in Missouri, introducing many from that county in Kentucky to the Northeast quadrant bound by the Mississippi and Missouri rivers.

71 "Daniel Boone," Wikipedia Foundation, accessed 2023.-2024.

The Allure of Marion County, Missouri

Before the two Clark brothers and others who pursued Missouri's promised lands, early settlement by pioneers into the Upper Louisiana west of the Mississippi River dates to the 1760s, when French explorers began establishing a fur trade in service to the Louisiana Fur Company in St. Louis. That settlement was founded in 1764 as a city by Pierre Laclede Liguest and his stepson Auguste Chouteau. France's governor for the territory awarded early Mississippi River and Louisiana Territory explorers permits to work in the area west of the Mississippi River and north of the Missouri River.[72]

In 1792, Maturin Bouvet, a member of Pierre Laclede Liguest's exploration party, traveled up the Mississippi with a handful of other men to search for opportunities that might yield rewards. They ventured into a stream pouring out of what is today's Salt River in Ralls County, directly below Marion County. There, Bouvet found a salt spring.[73] Bouvet returned to St. Louis to gather men and supplies, recognizing an opportunity to mine salt to sell in the southern areas of the Louisiana territory.

Bouvet's team constructed a salt furnace and warehouse at the mouth of the river. He named the complex of residence, furnace, and warehouse *the Bastion*. The salt was hauled from the spring overland by wagons and livestock rather than attempting to traverse the difficult, winding Salt River. Bouvet's Bastion was constructed on Bay de Charles, a settlement begun in 1795, "a little south of the mouth of Clear Creek" on the north side of Hannibal.[74] His operation faced several interruptions, including several attacks on his warehouse and factory by indigenous people, attributed

---

72 Later, permits were awarded by Spain's appointed governors over the Louisiana territory during 1763-1803: St. Louis was transferred to Spanish rule in 1770.

73 This was about twelve miles west of the village of New London that was platted in the early 1800s.

to the Sac.

In 1817, several men from Bourbon County, Kentucky (Edward Whaley, Aaron Foreman, Joseph Foreman, Aaron Foreman, Jr., and David Adams), traveled by foot and canoe to reach Northeast Missouri, having heard it to be flush with wild game, creeks, streams, forests and rolling hills for grazing. Witnessing this bounty, Whaley and the Foremans decided this area was promising for settlement and made homes there. Additional residents from Bourbon and Marion County, Kentucky, began their quest to settle in Marion County, Missouri, and its surroundings after hearing about this flourishing region.[75] By 1818, Marion was surveyed into townships with range and section measures. A large influx of settlers arrived there in 1819 to pursue opportunities, traveling either by the Ohio River then up the Mississippi, or the overland route with wagons through Indiana and Illinois, crossing the Mississippi at St. Louis.

The first recorded settlement in Marion County was "North and South Rivers" or "Two Rivers." For people residing between that region and St. Louis, it was known as "Two Rives [sic] Country." Many settled along South River, bringing their families and slaves.[76] The adjacent Ralls County was also established at that time (previously, Marion and Ralls were part of one county). A church building was constructed in 1821 in South River and means for education of the young was provided. The towns of Palmyra and nearby Hannibal soon were platted in 1822. Palmyra was

---

74 Liberty Township, where it empties into the Mississippi River. Historical accounts indicate a French explorer, Father Louis Hennepin, was first to come to Marion on behalf of the French government in 1680. Additional notes on the early days of the region are found in *A Mirror of Hannibal.* (Bacon, 1905)

75 Mahan, *Marion County, Missouri, History,* 1884.

76 This is where the Clarks and VanSchoiacks began their lives in Missouri. With Missouri admitted to the United States as a slave state by way of the Missouri Compromise of 1821, slave-owning Kentuckians would find it attractive to pursue prosperity there, bringing enslaved chattel with them. One Clark family account claims the Clark slaves were released in Kentucky; this is not certain (Clark, R.M. *The Genealogy of Our Parentage,* 1903).

a site for Indian camps in the early days. Camps of Sac among the large numbers of emigrants pouring in from Kentucky intermingled peacefully and frequently, yet the United States government was well into action to clear the Indigenous people from lands the young nation desired for expansion through westward settlement.

The Great Kentucky Exodus and the Dark Years

Kentuckian Moses Duncan Bates is recorded as the founder of Hannibal, Missouri. Bates, who surveyed Marion County, first settled on a large spring on South River. He then, in 1819, along with his wife Martha Gash Bates, whom he married while in St. Genevieve, built a log cabin at today's Main and Bird streets in Hannibal. Marion was officially made a county of Missouri in 1827, after which the nearby indigenous people moved away. By 1830, Marion County was well established, its residents cutting roads through forests and valleys to connect the settlements. Lumber was plentiful. Palmyra incorporated that year with the County's population having increased to 4,840 people; Hannibal's population was only around thirty.[77]

When listing the influences on Marion County, Missouri, the name Col. William Muldrow is among them. In 1821, Muldrow took ownership of the grounds of Bouvet's salt enterprise, the Bastion, that had been

---

77 The population of Hannibal by 1840 has been reported in one historic document to be 450 and in other places 1,024 [Powers, Mathew and Clio Admin. "Hock Building." Clio: Your Guide to History. October 30, 2022, theclio.com/entry/158367]. Notably, many of the early settlers succumbed to disease; the population might have been larger if the advantages of science were known and accessible.

destroyed. He rebuilt the factory and commenced operations but could not compete against the large number of salt-making enterprises operating in Ralls, St. Charles, and St. Louis counties. The market for salt mines became saturated as capitalists in Eastern Missouri, including Daniel Boone's sons, Nathan and Daniel Morgan Boone, who in 1805 established salt lick mining operations in Howard County along the Missouri River, attracted many to the northeast portion of Missouri and beyond. Because of this, Muldrow's competition was fierce, and he had to forego mining salt. However, this was not Muldrow's first enterprise to encounter collapse. Although he sold his salt works in 1826, he pursued other ways to advance settlement of the Northeast Missouri counties.

Muldrow envisioned great industry along the Mississippi River and sought a population to fuel it. In particular, Muldrow promoted his development of *Marion City,* "the Metropolis of the West," platted along the river six miles north of the site of Hannibal. This business venture included several investors and partners and developed rapidly. Many emigrants to Marion City came from the New England states, traveling down the Ohio to reach Missouri, while others from Virginia traveled Boone's Cumberland Gap route through the mountains into Kentucky or overland through Indiana and Illinois.

Born in Muldrow Hill, Marion County, Kentucky, on April 12, 1797, William Muldrow was said to have persuaded 300 families to relocate to Marion County, Missouri, between 1830 and 1835—the period when the Clarks traveled to the Upper Mississippi.[78,79]

After living in Kentucky for three decades and establishing themselves there, two of John Clark's four sons—James and John, with their wives and children—ventured to Marion County, Missouri, in 1830,

---

78 Marion is named for Francis Marion, a Brigadier General in the Revolutionary War ("The Swamp Fox") from South Carolina.

79 This is according to the perspective of Hannibal resident Thomas H. Bacon, born in 1839, author of the history segment for the book, *A Mirror of Hannibal* (1905).

along with the VanSchoiacks and other families.[80] They traveled overland through Illinois, crossing the Mississippi River at St. Louis. Arriving in the fall, they first settled on a farm in an area called Woodland.[81] Immediately, the Clark and VanSchoiack families constructed a log cabin for all to inhabit before the depths of the great snow fell upon them that winter.

It was in 1831 that Marion College was founded in the Marion County settlement of Philadelphia. The college succeeded in attracting highly educated instructors of classical education, offering a focus on agriculture and living by a Presbyterian Christian philosophy. There were three campuses to serve the settlers of Marion County and greater Northeast Missouri.[82] By 1835, the college achieved twenty-five percent of its goal to attract 425 students. Half of the ninety students it attracted by 1835 were from Missouri and the other half from sixteen other states. Plans for a medical school and a college for women were announced.

Records show Dr. David Clark, the two Clark brothers' uncle, was

---

80 According to the family history *The Genealogy of our Parentage*, compiled by Robert M. Clark in 1905, the Clark and Vanschoiacke families sold their property in Woodland, Marion County, to the settlement of South River, then "in the summer of 1836 sold out to a Mr. Jack Shell of Kentucky that was during the time of the Muldrow and Ely boom" (Clark, R.M., 1905). Ezra Styles Ely was Muldrow's partner in the development of land near Hannibal and Palmyra and launched institutions of learning, including Hannibal College in Philadelphia, Marion County. James Clark later purchased property near Ely Station alongside the rails of the Hannibal-St. Joseph railroad. The segment (below) about the Clarks and VanSchoiack families addresses variations in surname spellings.

81 This is believed to be where Woodland Station was built along the Hannibal and St. Joseph railroad line (later becoming the Quincy Railroad and other names). After weathering that difficult season in South River Township, southwest of Palmyra, the VanSchoiack family settled in the northeast corner of Monroe County, about four miles south of the village of Hunnewell, which is part of Shelby County, west of Marion County. (Clark, R.M., 1905)

82 Notably, women and persons of color are registered in the college's church registry of 1841, including Margaret L. Clark and Josephine Clark in addition to David Clark. [*Marion College Church Register*, Missouri Digital Heritage, Missouri State Library]

an advisor to the College. According to research conducted by Hannibal historian Goldena Howard in 1954, Dr. Clark, together with the College founders, claimed land north of Palmyra for raising cattle to support the college. Clark was charged with establishing means by which students could labor in the operations of the college in lieu of tuition to meet its expenses. This included managing cattle that could graze easily on the grassy Missouri fields and other farming chores.[83] The cattle would be sold to markets in St. Charles and St. Louis as well as farther south along the Mississippi's shores. Unfortunately, Clark arranged to bring the cattle to Northeast Missouri just before winter. With the cattle hungry for grazing and that being the year of the great 1831 deep snow, covering all grass, the cattle could not survive the hardships of the weather and lack of stored hay.

There was more to challenge the early Marion County pioneer families at that time. In 1833 and again in 1835, a cholera epidemic took the lives of eighteen percent of the Marion County population. In 1835, many settlers evacuated to more spacious quarters, trying to escape close proximity to others and reduce the chance of infection. Several in the Clark family were taken to their graves by this contagious disease. Symptoms of the disease appeared quickly; dying was painful and soon following. By sheer volume of the deceased and fear of infection, most were buried without time for coffin or ceremony.

In the neighboring county of Monroe, the village of Florida was formed, attracting as many as one hundred settlers by the time the Clemens family relocated there from Tennessee. They came to take advantage of its ample timber, good soil, waterways, and the promise of mining salt. In the spring of 1835, Samuel Clemens' father, John Marshall Clemens, along with his young family, left no fewer than 75,000 undeveloped acres

---

83 Howard, Godena (Mrs. Oliver Howard). "Muldrow's Marion City," *Hannibal Courier-Post*, August 23, 1954.

of land he owned[84] outside of Jamestown, Tennessee, to join members of his wife's family, who first visited Missouri in the late 1820s, settling in Florida by 1834. Samuel Langhorn Clemens was born in Florida on November 30, 1835.

In 1837, the nation experienced a great financial recession that would last until 1840. By 1839, Florida had seen nearly all its hopes for growth succumb. Many left Florida and pursued opportunities in Hannibal, which had grown to a population of 3000 through an influx of trades and industries. The Clemens family sold their property in 1839, when Samuel was four, and headed east. With proceeds from selling his Florida investments and through borrowing more cash, Clemens purchased buildings along the northeast corner of Hannibal's Main and Hill streets. He also invested in various endeavors that, too, would know hardship. Sam, on the other hand, experienced a decade of adventure, trials, and social awareness as a child coming of age in the active river town.

The late 1830s and 1840s were called "the dark years." This was not only because the national economy faced a financial crisis in 1837 after the U. S. national war debt was paid off—at last—in January 1835, but there was also disease. A plague of cholera impacted business and the national economy as it did during the era of seeking California gold. The dire situation provided a great religious awakening to thrive, with government entities called for days of prayer to be observed. Some believed it was the sins of the nation, such as slavery and strong drink, to bring on the devastating health conditions. Those decades (and decades after) also were busy, however, with plans for building railroads and all the politics of westward development that entailed, including establishing two capital

---

84 This land, in in Fentress County, Tennessee, remained in the Clemens family for many decades. It later befell Sam and his brother Orion to sell the hilly, rocky land that their father had purchased as a security for his family, believing the land offered many resources that could provide financial security for his offspring after he was gone. Alas, by this time, as titles to the portions of the property changed hands improperly over the decades, there was from the original purchase much less remaining for the Clemens brothers to sell, and what remained was of little practical value, its coal value not yet realized (Kaplan 2003, 8).

cities for Marion County: one in Palmyra and one in Hannibal. Eventually, a rail line ran from Hannibal through small Missouri towns to St. Joseph. It would follow the traces and trails cut long ago by Indian nations, trails that also served as a path for those pursuing gold in California.

The Rush is On

The U. S. military had known of mineral and metal wealth in California and took steps to possess it through conquest. Knowledge of this potential wealth for the average, ambitious man spread quickly across the country beginning in the fall of 1848. Word of gold found in the hills of California spilled across Northeast Missouri. Without delay, in early 1849, Muldrow formed a mining company to investigate, meeting with Capt. John Sutter of the famed initial gold strike near Sacramento.[85] These two formed a business partnership through which thousands of acres along the Russian River were purchased. Alas, Muldrow and Sutter parted ways after the first months of working in partnership, their contract disputed in courts for years; ultimately, and again, Muldrow lost that fortune invested in the promises of California. Muldrow worked in California for twenty years, not returning to Marion County until October 1869.

According to various historians in the nineteenth and twentieth

---

85 Horner (2006), 244-245. Sutter came to America from Baden, Germany, in 1834. His first three years were spent in Missouri, becoming a trader along the Santa Fe Trail that begins north of Boonville in Central Missouri, then turns south at Independence to Santa Fe, New Mexico. One might assume Muldrow made acquaintance with Sutter from his early days in Missouri before Sutter pursued adventures west. Sutter settled in the Sacramento area in 1839 and named the American River there—which provided a rich mining field for the Missourians who followed a decade later.

centuries, Hannibal's Samuel Clemens (Mark Twain) knew Muldrow. Some have said Muldrow was the inspiration for Twain's fictional character, Col. Mulberry Sellers, an adventurous man who creates a boom town called "Napoleon" so he might "conquer the commercial world." This is easily interpreted as a twist on Col. Muldrow and Marion City. Col. Sellers appears in the 1892 Twain novel, The American Claimant, "a comedy of mistaken identities." Although some Marion County historians believed Col. Sellers was based on Muldrow, it is in early drafts of Twain's autobiography that Twain explains how Sellers was based on his wife's cousin, James Lampton. It was Lampton, Twain explains, who was always dreaming of an enterprise that was "sure to be profitable" and frequently used the expression, "there's millions in it," as the fictional character Col. Sellers does in the play Gilded Age.[86]

Additionally, Muldrow's Marion City and Muldrow himself have been suggested as the inspiration for a work by Charles Dickens that tells of a city named Eden.[87] Dickens visited Missouri in 1842 when Marion College was sold, and possibly a time Dickens might have been introduced to the topic.

In 1848, Samuel Clemens, whose father had died the year before, curtailed his formal schooling and began working for the Hannibal Missouri Courier newspaper as an apprentice. He was thirteen. The letters the Marion County argonauts sent to citizens of Missouri added to the gold fever, and a flood of its residents quickly gathered supplies to go west in 1849 and the years following. Others in Marion County who journeyed to California in 1849 include The Rev. Benjamin Franklin Stevens. He sent letters to his wife with instructions for sharing his reports with the Hannibal Journal.[88]

In its May 3, 1849, edition, The Hannibal Journal included a list of people from the Marion County area who were in California.

---

86 Twain, Mark. *Autobiography,* Volume 1. H.E. Smith, Editor. (Los Angeles: University of California Press, 2013), 1: 55, 206

87 Los Angeles Herald, "Dickens' Eden is sold" (*Chicago Chronicle*). Volume 30, No. 151, March 6, 1903.

88 Stevens kept a detailed diary of people, places, and events. This lengthy diary can be found online. The Stevens account was vetted and edited by J. Hurley Hagood. It lists many names of Missourians who went to California and describes conditions of the journey—fore, during, and upon return.

These individuals traveled in small groups, called a "mess." Seventy-four individuals are listed, some taking their families (who are not included in that tally). Among those named are those who formed companies to mine in California or who were part of a company. The list notes those who sent reports back to Missouri, including Capt. Archibald S. Robards and his twelve-year-old son, John, who was a childhood and life-long friend of Sam Clemens. The father and son journeyed to California in 1849 with a company of fifteen men from Hannibal.[89]

Not yet coming-of-age, an impressionable Samuel Clemens witnessed Hannibal's rapid decline among the male portion of its population. As much as one-third of its men scrambled to venture west upon learning of gold flowing in California's streams and creeks. Sam Clemens was not yet fourteen when Robards' team of adventurers launched West. "We were all on hand to gaze and envy when [John Robards] returned, two years later, in unimagined glory—for he had traveled," Clemens (Twain) wrote in his autobiographical notes. "None of us had ever been forty miles from home. But he had crossed the continent. He had been in the gold mines, that fairyland of our imagination," he recalled. "We would have sold our souls to Satan for the privilege of trading places with him."[90]

Spotswood Williams went to California and sent reports about life in the gold mines, which Bob and Sam Clark read in local papers in 1850. Additional published letters from Marion miners include those of Edward Murphy, who reported many details about the areas where Missourians were working, the routes they took, and the settlements they built. William Hubbard went west from the Hannibal region with eight men and two wagons. By these accounts, the Clark brothers and others were inspired to join other Missourians in the fields.

As Robert Mason Clark notes in his memoirs, reading the letters in

---

89 According to his friend Sam Clemens, John RoBards later chose to capitalize the B of his surname as an aggrandizement so that it might suggest an aristocratic heritage (Twain, *Autobiography* Vol. I, 611)

90 Twain, Mark. *Autobiography*, Volume One. H.E. Smith, Editor. (Los Angeles: University of California Press, 2013), 401.

the newspaper inspired him and additional Northeast Missouri enterprising men to follow their ambitions and pursuits, resulting in continual westward expansion. The stories from the Robards company, the Clark brothers, and others among the 1851-1853 adventurers conveyed accounts of success, adventure, failures, and danger. While the Clark brothers were mining in California, Samuel Clemens read the accounts of other miners' success and adventure coming into Northeast Missouri newspapers. In January 1851, Sam Clemens, at age 15, began working for his brother Orion, who had started the *Hannibal Western Union* paper and in 1852 obtained the *Hannibal Journal*.

In 1853, a year after Robert Clark returned from California, Samuel Clemens left Hannibal at age seventeen to begin his life of adventures, He began as a journeyman printer in St. Louis and continued to other cities, including New York, Philadelphia, and Washington. When Samuel's brother, Orion, was appointed Secretary for the Nevada Territory in 1861 by Abraham Lincoln—for whom Orion had campaigned—Sam accompanied his brother during the stagecoach trip west.

Beginning in 1862, Sam Clemen's lifelong pursuit of adventure and travel included an attempt at silver mining in Nevada, but without success. By July of that year, Clemens began to leverage his writing talents. It was among and for the Nevada miners and the capitalizing people who boldly ventured west to serve them that Sam Clemens provided entertainment by creating stories sold to the *Virginia City Territorial Enterprise* newspaper. In 1863, he first penned the byline "Mark Twain," drawing upon his Northeast Missouri and Mississippi River heritage for inspiration.[91]

---

91 Twain, *Autobiography,* Vol I, 251; Vol II, 239, 567.

The Clark and VanSchoiack Families

The Clark lineage reveals a heritage steeped in progressive pursuits. The first Clark immigrant from England was John Clark (b. 1750), whose trans-Atlantic voyage brought him to Baltimore, Maryland, as a youth near the beginning of the Revolutionary War. John, along with his son, Samuel Clark (who married Sallie Fife) took advantage of opportunities in Kentucky.[92] The Clarks settled in Bourbon County (or the portion carved from that, namely Shannon River in Nicholas County) in the late 1700s. Another notable family that found promise by relocating to Kentucky was Robert (and Elisabeth Allen) VanSchoiack and their relatives.[93] John Clark and his wife had a daughter who married Josiah VanSchoiack in the Mason County area in Kentucky.[94]

The VanSchoiack family, of Dutch heritage (Utrecht, the Netherlands), originally settled in New York, farming 'outside the *wall*' of the early settlement on Manhattan (from which the name *Wall Street* derives), around

---

92 Not to be confused with the descendant Samuel Clark of this gold rush account.

93 Over time, descendants with the Vanschoiacke name [originally pronounced in Marion County as Van SKOYK] changed the spelling to Vanskike or Vanskyke and the pronunciation changed to VanSKIKE. In the Netherlands, from which the family emigrated, the name can be found as van Schaijck, although at least one offspring--William (1767-1841) born in New Jersey--wrote the name as VanSchoiack while each of his 6 siblings used one's own unique way: Van Schoyck, Van Schoick, Van Schaick, Van Schayk and even Van Sickle in various records. Schaijck is the name of a town in the Netherlands province of North Brabant. R.M. Clark, in his *The Genealogy of Our Parentage* (1905) used Vanschoiacke.

94 Mason County is named for George Mason of Virginia, who was a delegate to the 1787 Constitutional Convention and drafted the U.S. Bill of Rights, based on the Virginia Declaration of Rights which he wrote. The county was partitioned from Bourbon County in 1788, which was established in 1785 from Fayette County. Kentucky entered the Union in 1792.

the year 1650 according to VanSchoiack family historians. Today there are many things with the name "Van Schaick" in Albany and other areas of New York, many dating back to military achievements of the 1700s. An historic mansion and an island along the Hudson River are named after this family.

The VanSchoiacks settled in Maysville, Mason County, Kentucky, built that county's first brick house, and brought their Baptist faith with them. Several of the Clark and VanSchoiack offspring intermarried, including within the generation of California gold rush brothers, Robert and Samuel Clark. Their mother, Polly VanSchoiack, daughter of Robert and Elizabeth (Allen) VanSchoiack, was married to their father James Clark.

John Clark was converted to the Methodist faith "through the Wesley Meetings in London," inspired by Methodist founder and Anglican priest John Wesley.[95] In Kentucky, John Clark built on his farm a church, which he named Pisgah—the name of a mountain in the Biblical story of Moses, from which Moses viewed *the promised land.*

From sailing the Atlantic to sojourning land in harsh manner and conditions, becoming Northeast Missourians incurred dangers by both nature and man. Three generations preceding those taking the California Trail were encumbered with intense physical challenges, constant relocation, trepidation, and unsettling emotions in pursuit of improving their lot. Inspiration and lessons from these tests of human capacity of spirit, determination, and strength surely formed a legacy that inspired descending generations to pursue means of assuring their well-being.

---

95 Clark, Robert Mason. *"Genealogy of Our Parentage,"* Hunnewell, Missouri, 1904.

Bibliography

"An Account of Webber Creek." *Oakland Tribune*. Oakland, CA. July 14, 1946.

"El Dorado Gold." *Mountain Democrat*. Placerville, CA. June 12, 1997.

Ancestry, Rootsweb (affiliated with Ancestry.com). Online genealogical and historical resources; multiple contributors. Accessed 2011-2024. https://www.ancestry.com.

Bacon, Thomas H. *A Mirror of Hannibal*. Hannibal: C. P. Greene, Editor and Publisher, 1905.

Bright, Wm. *1500 California Place Names*. Berkeley, CA: University of California Press, 1998.

Broman, M. and Leadabrand, R. *California Ghost Town Trails*. Baldwin Park, CA: Gem Guides, 1985.

Clark, Robert M., *"The Genealogy of Our Parentage,"* 1905.

Clark, B. C. *Diary of a Journey from Missouri to California in 1849*. Missouri Historical Review, Vol. 23.1, October 1928. https://digital.shsmo.org/digital/collection/mhr/id/10527.

Dempsey, Terrell. *Searching for Jim*. Columbia, MO: University of Missouri Press, 2003.

Dunbar-Ortiz, Roxanne. *An Indigenous People's History of the United States*. Boston: Beacon Press, 2019.

Emigrant Trails West, Inc. *Journals; Trail Commentaries.* https://
emigranttrailswest.org.

Enzler, Jerry. *Trailblazer for the American West.* Norman, OK: University
of Oklahoma Press, 2021.

Finley, Newton Gleaves. *"Memoirs of Travel"* 1922. Edited submission to
Salt Lake City Family History Library by A. L Alderman, 1981.

Garey, Richard. *Hannibal at the Door.* Outskirts Press, 2017.

HeritageQuest. Online genealogical databases and historical resources.
Accessed 2023-2024. https://www.heritagequestonline.com.

Holcombe, R. I. *History of Marion County Missouri - 1884.* E.F. Perkins.
Reprint Brookhaven Press, 2000.

Holliday, J. S. *The World Rushed In: The California Gold Rush Experience.*
Norman, OK: University of Oklahoma Press, 1982.

Hornor, R. & Hornor, J. *The Golden Corridor.* Pilot Hill, CA: 19th
Century Books, 2005.

Hornor, R. & Hornor, J. *The Golden Highway.* Pilot Hill, CA: 19th
Century Books, 2006.

Hulbert, Archer Butler. *Forty-Niners.* Boston: Little Brown & Company,
1931.

Johnson, W.W. *The Forty-Niners.* New York: Time-Life Books, 1974.

Kaplan, Fred. *The Singular Mark Twain: A Biography.* New York: Random
House, 2003.

Kelly, Leslie A. *Traveling California's Gold Rush Country.* Helena, MT:
Falcon Guide, 1997.

Kennedy, Robert V. *Kennedy's 1860 St. Louis City Directory*. St. Louis, MO:
      Kennedy, R.V., 1860.

Larson, E. A website of maps and resources about the Overland Trail.
      https://over-land.com.

Library of Congress. *Directory of U.S. Newspapers in American Libraries*.
      Accessed 2020-2024. https://www.loc.gov/item/sn90061072/

McDougall Gordon, Mary, Editor. *Overland to California with the Pioneer
      Line: the Gold Rush Diary of Bernard J. Reid*. Stanford CA:
      Stanford University Press, 1983.

McNeil, Keith and Rusty. *Moving West Songs with historical narration*. WEM
      Records, 1989. https://www.wemrecords.com.

Missouri Digital Heritage, Marion College Church Register. *Register of
      the Church of Marion College, 1836-1857*. Missouri State Library,
      Jefferson City, Missouri. Accessed 2024. https://mdh.
      contentdm.oclc.org/digital/collection/moslpl/id/75/.

Missouri Historical Review. *"Diary of a Journey from Missouri to California
      in 1849,"* Ralph P. Bieber, editor. 23:1. October 1928.

Munkres, Robert. "Trail Facts about the Oregon and California Trails."
      Oregon-California Trails Association. Accessed 2024. https//
      octa-trails.org.

National Park Service, U.S. Department of the Interior. *National Historic
      Trails: Auto Tour Route Interpretive Guides*, 2012.

National Park Service, U.S. Department of the Interior. https://www.
      nps.gov/places.

Palmyra, Missouri Collection, 1829-1880. *Gold Rush articles of agreement
      A1177*. Missouri Historical Society Archives, St. Louis.

Perkins, E. F. *History of Marion County, Missouri*. St. Louis, MO, 1884. Reprint: Holcombe, R. I., editor. St. Louis: Brookhaven Press, 2000.

Reid, Bernard J. *Overland to California with the Pioneer Line*. Gordon, M. M., Editor. Stanford: Stanford University Press, 1983.

Robards, John L. *The Story of the Pioneer*. County History of Northeast Missouri, Walter Williams, editor. Chicago: Lewis Publishing Company, 1913.

Robinson, W.W. *Land in California*. Berkeley, CA: University of California Press, 1948.

Rogers, T.M. *Atlas map of Marion County, Missouri*. Quincy, IL: Rogers, T. M., 1875.

Sappington, Howard, Sappington, Sandy. *Pioneers: Old Bloomington Trail Links North Missouri*. Letter to Daviess County Historical Society, 2011. https://daviesscountyhistoricalsociety.com

Stevens, Rev. Benjamin Franklin. *The Journal of Rev. Benjamin Franklin Stevens; 1849 Journal of the Trip by Covered Wagon During the California Gold Rush*. Hickman Chase transcription. Hannibal, MO. Accessed 2023. https://hannibal.lib.mo.us/journal.htm.

Findagrave.com. online genealogical and historical resources. Tipton, Jim (founder). Accessed 2019-2024. https://www.findagrave. com.

Towle, Russell. *History of the North Fork of the American River*. North Fork of the American River (digital blog) August 12, 2008. Accessed 2024. https://northforktrails.blogspot.com.

Twain, Mark. *Autobiography. Volumes I and II*. University of California Press, 2013.

Vestal, Stanley. *Jim Bridger: Mountain Man.* University of Nebraska Press, 1970.

Weant, Kenneth E. *The 49ers: Articles about the 49er's in the Missouri Republican, Vol. 1&2. 1848-1850.* Arlington, TX: Kenneth E. Weant, 2004.

Weant, Kenneth E. *The Marian* [sic] *County 49'ers. Personal Letters, Obituaries and Articles about the California Gold Rush from The Missouri Whig 2 January 1849 to 22 December 1852.* Volume 3. Arlington, TX: Kenneth E. Weant. 2004.

Wikimedia Foundation. Wikipedia platform. Accessed 2011-2024. https://www.wikipedia.org/

Zorbas, Elane. *Fiddletown, From Gold Rush to Rediscovery.* Altadena, CA: Mythos Press. 1997.

Index

People

Places

Acknowledgments

Although this book is small, it took a team to get it in your hands. The following individuals and institutions played various roles that influenced this compilation and are here recognized.

Edna Clark Hoxworth realized the value of saving and sharing her grandfather's memoir. Without her vision and action, none of this would be read today.

Richard Clark and Shannon Hayes were critical in getting the Hoxworth pages and library microfilm photocopies into a digital format.

Anthony E. Patterson, who deeply believed in the value of resurrecting Robert Clark's Gold Rush memoir, applied his technical and language acumen early in the production of this compilation. His presence on the project as an editing partner was a great gift and continued to inspire as this collection of words reached completion.

Several people helped cleanse early drafts. They include Michael Oster, Dorothy Bailey, DeeDee Hoffman, Sue Stone, Vicki Fox, and travel writer Janice Branham. Editing advice from Becky Strickland, Donna Brodsky and Jessica Cissell resolved many questions that lingered. Any remaining errors are mine.

Gratitude goes to several esteemed historians, including Travis Boley, Association Manager of the Oregon-California Trails Association and former Executive Director of the Pony Express Museum in St. Joseph, who read this manuscript with appreciation and grace, and provided additional details about the trails; Northeast Missouri historians Terrell Dempsey and Richard Garey provided insight to those earlier days; members of the Saunders family—early settlers of Shelby County—opened doors to understanding the migration of Kentucky emigrants to the region surrounding Palmyra and Hannibal; genealogist Mia Adkins Fleegel, a descendant of Robert's brother Sam Clark, shared her knowledge of the Clark family and led me to the ancestral burial sites tucked deep in the backroads of Marion County, Missouri.

Staff at many libraries and historical societies, as well as knowledgeable sources on social media platforms, made this work easier and largely enjoyable; thank you.

Encouragement and knowledge from friends, writers, and fellow researchers helped move me toward completion of this project that either ran or dragged along for more than fifteen years. These include Merna Gill, A. Elizabeth Kurrus, Stephanie Binz, Tom Binz, Cherie Postill, Rebecca Peterson, and my siblings DeeDee, Vicki and Sue.

The encouraging and patient production support and skillful direction from book designer and author, Brad Cook of Broadsword Books, and from author and knowledgeable writing coach Jessica Mathews were invaluable, truly enabling this compilation to reach completion and binding.

Finally, I salute members of the Olin Wilson and Eva Mae Clark family, especially my husband James, as they were essential for this lengthy research and writing process to evolve from dream to reality.

I surely have failed to mention others who held a role in resurrecting Robert M. Clark's memoir; yet, their contributions are very much appreciated.

Marsha K. Clark

Clad so heavy in her native forests abounding in wild game and honey, the prairies adorned in summer time with native grass and set as with wild flowers.

Here, the wild deer loved to feed, sport, and play.

Here, the hunter's boy could sit and see the wild cranes, geese, brants, swim on the natural ponds and streams by the hundreds.

He could also hear
the chatter of the timid squirrel in the forest,
the cooing of the wild pigeon;
hear the whirl of pheasant's wing,
the call and gobble of the wild turkey,
the drum of the prairie chicken,
the whistle of the deer,
the cry of the wild cat,
and the howl of the big, black and gray wolf.

These were all familiar to him in those days.

Robert M. Clark, April 9, 1850, describing the lands of the Chariton River Bottom while seated next to his schooner during a rest stop in Macon County, Missouri, soon after having embarked on his journey west.

www.ingramcontent.com/pod-product-compliance
Lightning Source LLC
Chambersburg PA
CBHW041202150726
48006CB00016B/2082